HISTORIAN'S HANDBOOK

A Key to the Study and Writing of History
SECOND EDITION

WOOD GRAY

WITH THE COLLABORATION OF

William Columbus Davis	Elmer Louis Kayser
Roderic Hollett Davison	Robert Wayne Kenny
Richard Catlin Haskett	Myron Law Koenig
Charles Joseph Herber	Howard Maxwell Merriman
Peter Proal Hill	Ronald Bettes Thompson

The George Washington University

HOUGHTON MIFFLIN COMPANY · BOSTON

Quotations by permission of

Longmans, Green and Company for Mr. G. M. Trevelyan
Harcourt, Brace and Company for Mr. T. S. Eliot
Mrs. Eugene (Carlotta Monterey) O'Neill
AAUP Bulletin, Mr. William E. Britton, and Judge Learned Hand
The New Yorker and Mr. James Thurber
Mr. Charles M. Schulz and United Features Syndicate
Courtesy of *The Washington Post and Times Herald*

ABOUT THIS HANDBOOK

Many books discuss historical methodology. A considerable number of them are cited in the footnotes of the pages that follow. Among such works this *Handbook* is unique in the degree to which it is both comprehensive and concise. Its purpose is to introduce the college freshman and general reader to the nature of history, with suggestions as to how he may study it effectively; to guide the advanced student through the preparation of a term paper or thesis; and to offer the practicing historian a convenient reference manual.

This undertaking has benefited at many points from criticisms and suggestions from Douglass G. Adair of Claremont College, Thomas A. Bailey and David M. Potter of Stanford University, Ray Allen Billington, Franklin D. Scott, and Paul A. Schipp of Northwestern University, Stetson Conn, Helen Brents Joiner, and Lida Mayo of the Army historical section, Richard N. Current of the University of Wisconsin, William Lloyd Fox of Montgomery Junior College, Frank Freidel of Harvard University, Andrew Gregorovich of McMaster University, Maurice Christopher Hollis of Frome, Somersetshire, William T. Hutchinson of the University of Chicago, Edward C. Kirkland of Bowdoin College, Melvin L. Kohn of the National Institutes of Health, Leonard W. Labaree of Yale University, Arthur S. Link of Princeton University, Mary Macgillivray of the Canadian Embassy, Horace S. Merrill of the University of Maryland, Jeannette P. Nichols of the University of Pennsylvania, Forrest C. Pogue of the George C. Marshall Research Foundation, Charles Poore of *The New York Times,* Julius W. Pratt of the University of Buffalo, Marin Pundeff of San Fernando Valley State College, Carroll Quigley and Salvatore L. Costabile of Georgetown University, Wayne D. Rasmussen of the U. S. Department of Agriculture, Richard Rovere of *The New Yorker,* Howard Smith and George O. Kent of the Department of State, Lionel Trilling of Columbia University, Walter L. Wakefield of State University College, Potsdam, New York, Bennett H. Wall of the University of Kentucky, Wilcomb E. Washburn of the Smithsonian Institution, and Louis B. Wright of the Folger Shakespeare Library. Of the staff of the Library of Congress, Francisco Aguilera, Roy P. Basler, Gladys R. Carpenter, James B. Childs, Helen Field Conover, John C. Crawford, John J. DePorry, Johannes L. Dewton, Stewart Dickson, John M. Hunt, Mary Ellis Kahler, Robert H. Land, Frank E. Louraine, David C. Mearns, Donald H. Mugridge, C. Percy Powell, Daniel J. Reed, Walter W. Ristow, William Sartain, George A. Schwegmann, Jr., Fred Shelley, Osamu Shimizu, Lillian Takeshita, John H. Thaxter, Willard Webb,

Frank W. Wilson, and T'ung-li Yüan and of the National Archives, Katherine H. Davidson, W. Neil Franklin, Anne Harris Henry, Albert H. Leisenger, Jr., Ken Munden, and Leonard A. Rapport, and of the George Washington University Library, John Russell Mason, Anna Virginia Appich, Hugh Yancey Bernard, Jr., Mona Byrd, Mercy Stoner McCurdy, Joanne Thompson Monk, Susan Pierce Murray, Edith Sewall Phillips, Alice Sheftel, and Mary Elizabeth Thompson have all been particularly helpful. I am under special obligations to Guy Stanton Ford and Boyd C. Shafer, former and present editors of *The American Historical Review* and to Mary Rulkotter Dearing and Patricia M. Fox, former and present assistant editors. Additional suggestions and corrections for the improvement of the *Handbook* will be welcomed in the hope that it may ultimately be possible to establish a standard form of citation and usage best suited to the needs of historical scholarship everywhere.

The needs and wishes of students in some fifty of my research seminar courses have provided guidance in the compression of the material contained in this *Handbook* into its present form. A number of students, including Dean C. Allard, Jr., Jean Rice Anderson, Elisabeth Griffith Bernheisel, Dorothy Z. Brewer, Elizabeth A. Buser, Rachel MacIntyre Dach, Clarice R. Felder, Mary Grover, Dermott V. Hickey, Thomas Page Johnson, Carol Koyen Kammen, Virginia L. Lee, Henry F. Beaumont Martin, Sandra Lee Myers, George Orlove, Eloise Randolph Page, David J. Patterson, Frank J. Redding, Rosa D. Weiner, and Chloe Wellingham suggested specific improvements on the basis of various preliminary drafts. All approved the concentrated and didactic form in which the work was finally cast — "a five hundred page book in fifty pages" — in which sentences must sometimes do the work of paragraphs and paragraphs that of chapters. They united in urging all future students to read closely and to digest carefully, even at times virtually to memorize, what they read in order to derive the fullest possible benefit. Remember that in the process of "boiling down" it is principally water that is removed, leaving the solid substance undiminished. This *Handbook* is intended to be studied and followed as you would the directions in a cookbook or a laboratory manual, in which inattention is likely to result in an embarrassing failure, or even an explosion. *Don't skim!*

My colleagues whose names appear on the title page have at every stage provided suggestions, criticisms, and, in particular, aid in the compiling of bibliographies in fields unfamiliar to the author. The help given by William C. Davis, Howard Maxwell Merriman, and Ronald B. Thompson requires special acknowledgment. My colleagues John W. Brewer, Wolfgang H. Kraus, Hugh L. LeBlanc, and H. Rowland Ludden of the Department of Political Science, Gust A. Ledakis of the Law School (with additional assistance from Miles Gray, of Wood, Gray, and Wood of Springfield, Illinois, and from Peter Barton Hutt of Covington and Burling of Washington, D. C.), Philip H. Highfill of the Department of English, John F. Latimer of the Department of Classical Languages and Literatures, and Helen Bates Yakobson of the Department of Slavic Languages and Literatures rendered special assistance. James B. Childs and John H. Thaxter of the Library of Congress gave valued aid in cutting a way through the tangled thickets of government-document citation, and Jean Rice Anderson and S. Lee Siebenlist Nye brought both patience and alertness to the preparation of the second edition of the *Handbook*. Lester Kruger Born of the Library of Congress provided information on programs, and hopes for union catalogues of manuscript sources. None of the above, however, is chargeable with any remaining shortcomings in either the conception or execution of this work, the responsibility for which is inescapably my own.

WOOD GRAY

WASHINGTON, D. C.

CONTENTS

CONTENTS

Page   *Page*

Symbols Commonly Used in Proofreading   Back Cover

AN INTRODUCTION TO THE NATURE OF HISTORY

Time present and time past
Are both perhaps present in time future,
And time future contained in time past.

T. S. Eliot, *Four Quartets*, "Burnt Norton."

Tyrone: Mary! For God's sake, forget the past!
Mary: Why? How can I? The past is the present, isn't it? It's the future, too.
We all try to lie out of that but life won't let us.

Eugene O'Neill, *Long Day's Journey into Night*,
Act II, scene 2.

History leads to understanding and wisdom. It is a road beset with pitfalls for the untutored and unwary, but the vistas expand as you journey upward and at the end a treasure house awaits if you have the necessary keys.

An early stumbling block may be the friend (or so you had thought him) who seeks to discourage you from devoting time to the study of history that you could be spending on purely "practical" subjects. This self-satisfied Mr. Know-All would probably have sufficient good sense to consult a properly trained expert about any such relatively simple matter as a lawsuit or business problem, a sick body or malfunctioning automobile, or a leaking roof; but he is likely to be in the habit of confidently appealing to the "lessons of history" as irrefutable proof for whatever point of view he may be advocating, without being qualified to pass a freshman examination in the field.[1] In the pages that follow you may find answers for him if he is not past saving.

You will also discover that, while it is comparatively easy to describe the methods of historical research, they may prove to be complex and obdurate when one begins to apply them to a specific investigation.

1. What is history? There are a number of interlocking definitions. Most commonly the word is used to mean one of the following or perhaps a combination of two, or all three, of them:

---

[1] Sir Leslie Stephen (*Social Rights and Duties*, I, 129), observed, "The Catholic and the Protestant, the Conservative and the Radical, the Individualist and the Socialist, have equal facility in proving their own doctrines with arguments, which habitually begin, 'All history shows.' Printers should be instructed always to strike out that phrase as an **erratum**; and to substitute, 'I choose to take for granted.'" Charles A. Beard listed a number of facile clichés of this type favored by editorialists and protagonists for partisan and economic interests (Social Science Research Council, Committee on Historiography, *Theory and Practice in Historical Study* . . . . SSRC, Bulletin 54, New York: SSRC, c. 1946, p. 4), to which we might add such other habitual offenders as military leaders and taxi drivers, and even in their careless moments, professors and students. This bulletin of 188 pages includes a reading list on historiography and the philosophy of history selected by Ronald Bettes Thompson.

1

a. Happening. In one sense history is everything that has occurred, or has been thought, from the beginning of time through the last elapsed instant. Available data, however, are essentially limited to the period of three to five billion years during which the physical universe has assumed its present form. Biological history may extend over the last third of that period, but its beginning is difficult to fix because the earliest forms of life lacked the structure that would enable them to leave fossilized remains. The human era, a brief one against this larger background but vast when measured against a single lifetime, may go back a million years or more. During most of his career man has been a savage who searched for food and shelter as nature provided them, much in the manner of other animals. He rose to the level of barbarism when he learned to domesticate some of those animals and to cultivate plants. Only within the last one per cent of his existence has he discovered the civilized practices of specialization and the exchange of goods and services which have afforded him more and more time to devote to other things than mere subsistence. In this foreshortened span of time the rapidity of change has been greatly accelerated, and diverse civilizations have come into being and passed into limbo. During the past five hundred years world trade has served increasingly to make all men interdependent and to lead them in the direction of a single world civilization. In the last two centuries man has gone so far in unlocking the secrets of mechanics and natural energy that he seems to be speeding toward a crossroad where he will either go on to realize his age-old hopes or destroy every form of life on earth. His next step will depend largely on how well he has mastered the lessons of his past experience.[2]

b. Record. Only a small proportion of all the things that happen leaves any permanent record. At first glance history-as-happening may seem to dwarf utterly history-as-record, the only material which the student of history has to work with. Fortunately men have long made conscious efforts to preserve the evidence of what they have had reason to believe to be the most important occurrences not only of their own time but of antecedent periods. With his faithful co-workers, the archivist and the librarian, the historian spends much of his time searching for new evidence and making it freely available for study. Like the paleontologist who can reconstruct a skeleton from a few fragments, the trained historian can recreate much of past society from a relatively small number of clues. The evidence includes physical survivals, such as buildings and artifacts unearthed by archaeologists. About five thousand years ago, shortly before the building of the Egyptian pyramids, the growing complexity of economic and political activity in ancient Mesopotamia and Egypt led to the invention of writing. It is with the period since that date that the bulk of historical study, as it is normally defined, is concerned. The development of printing in the Western world some five hundred years ago greatly magnified

---

2 Every student of history should own George Gamow, *Biography of the Earth* (Mentor Books, c. 1941; also new ed., Viking, c. 1959), Rachel Louise Carson, *The Sea Around Us* (Mentor Books; New York: New American Library, c. 1951), and Vere Gordon Childe, *What Happened in History* (New York: Pelican Books, Inc., c. 1946) — all inexpensive reprints — for an introduction to the beginning of the universe and man. See also Carleton Stevens Coon, *The Story of Man* . . . (New York: Alfred A. Knopf, Inc., 1954), Weston LaBarre, *The Human Animal* (Chicago: University of Chicago Press, 1954), Ralph Linton, *The Tree of Culture* (New York: Alfred A. Knopf, Inc., 1955), and Norman John Berrill, *Man's Emerging Mind* . . . (New York: Dodd, Mead & Co., c. 1955). Last two also paperbound.

the documentary record and the chances of its survival, serving in this respect to mark off the modern age from all that preceded it. In our own time photographic and phonographic devices have further increased the ease of record making, although telephonic communication has tended to eliminate certain types of written material that are valuable sources for earlier periods.

c. Field of study. Out of all the varied types of records and remains preserved from the past, men have been able to piece together the outlines of their ancestral experience, fitting them into patterns of chronological sequence, location, and topical organization which offer us a better chance to understand ourselves and the world we live in.

Even primitive man sought to commemorate the experiences of his tribe in sagas and legends. At about the halfway point between the beginning of written records and the present time, Herodotus and Thucydides brought to history a spirit of truth and a deepened conception of the relationship between causes and results that raised the subject so far above earlier chronicles written merely to glorify some monarch or city that one might justifiably capitalize it as History. Both men wrote as exiles — which in a sense every historian must do in order to achieve the objectivity and breadth of vision that are demanded by the obligations of his calling. Following the decline of classical civilization, the mind of the Middle Ages was in some respects antithetical to the spirit of true history. The rationalist disposition of the 18th century Enlightenment once more directed men's attention to the need for comprehensive historical study. One of its fruits, after the cataclysmic quarter-century of the French Revolution and Napoleonic period, was the rise in Germany of "scientific" history as an academic discipline with full status. In 1825 at the University of Berlin Professor Leopold von Ranke began to inculcate systematic methods for the evaluation of documents, and set before his students the ideal of re-creating the past "wie es eigentlich gewesen ist" (as it actually happened).

In the United States the study of history as a major part of higher education is a little over a century old. Earlier it was taught as a rather incidental subject — although for a decade after 1839 Jared Sparks occupied the newly established McLean chair of history at Harvard before assuming the presidency of that institution. In 1857 Andrew Dickson White, after graduate study in Germany (to which he would later return as our diplomatic representative), became professor of history at the University of Michigan; and in 1881, after he had become president of Cornell, he set up for Moses Coit Tyler (who also laid the basis for the academic study of American literature) the first professorship of American history. White's successor at Michigan, Charles Kendall Adams, introduced in 1869 the German type of seminar course — the historian's equivalent of the scientist's laboratory course. Seminars soon appeared also at Johns Hopkins University under Herbert Baxter Adams, at Harvard under Henry Adams, at Columbia under John W. Burgess, and elsewhere. In 1892 a famous German professor, Hermann Eduard von Holst, came to the United States to be head of the department of history at the University of Chicago.[3]

---

[3] Two discerning recent commentaries by leading European historians are Pieter Geyl, *Use and Abuse of History* (New Haven, Conn.: Yale University Press, 1955) and Herbert Butterfield, *Man on His Past: The Study of the History of Historical Scholarship* (Cambridge: Cambridge University Press, 1955). There have been a number of extended treatises by United States historians tracing the development of historiography. Most ambitious to date is James

In September, 1884, forty men (including Andrew D. White, Charles K. Adams, and Herbert B. Adams) met at Saratoga Springs to establish the American Historical Association. *The American Historical Review,* a quarterly covering every field of human history, began to appear in 1895. The first and long-time editor of the *AHR* was John Franklin Jameson, who also fathered the National Archives, the annual bibliography of *Writings on American History* (see Chapter 2, paragraph I-1-c, below), and the *Dictionary of American Biography* (Ch. 2, par. I-6-a). By 1900 the AHA had grown to a membership of sixteen hundred. Now numbering some ten thousand — about three-fourths of them college and university instructors and professors — it serves to integrate the work of other historical societies in almost every section and state and in many counties and cities. The oldest of them, the Massachusetts Historical Society, dates from 1791. Altogether these societies publish over a hundred historical journals. They welcome students (for whom many of them offer special rates), school teachers, and the general public as members. Virtually all of the more than eighteen hundred institutions of higher education in the United States offer courses in history. Some departments of history have nearly fifty members on the teaching staff. Other nations have similar, if less elaborate, organizations and academic programs. There may be approximately fifteen thousand professional historians in the world apart from those teaching at the secondary school level, more than one-half of them in the United States.[4]

Even more impressive is the fact that the profession, particularly in the last generation and wherever its members are free from outside compulsion, has approached substantial agreement on major issues — while leaving each individual scholar entirely free to proffer new or modified interpretations derived from an objective re-examination of the evidence. Although prejudice, like fear in battle, is a natural human weakness, both can be brought under control by proper training and the realization that they will bring condemnation by one's fellows — an analogy in which intentional falsification would be equivalent to overt disloyalty. Exaggeration of the difficulty of achieving objectivity may be only an attempt to excuse oneself for not making the necessary effort.

Westfall Thompson and Bernhard J. Holm, *A History of Historical Writing* (2 vols.; New York: Macmillan Co., 1942). Briefer treatments are Matthew A. Fitzsimons, Alfred G. Pundt, and Charles E. Nowell, eds., *The Development of Historiography* (Harrisburg, Pa.: Stackpole Co., c. 1954) and Harry Elmer Barnes, *A History of Historical Writing* (rev. ed.; New York: Dover Publications, 1961; paperbound). Michael Kraus, *The Writing of American History* (Norman: University of Oklahoma Press, c. 1954), Harvey Wish, *The American Historian . . .* (New York: Oxford University Press, 1960), and David D. VanTassel, *Recording America's Past . . . , 1607–1884* (Chicago: University of Chicago Press, 1960) trace developments in the United States. William Thomas Hutchinson, ed., *The Marcus W. Jernegan Essays in American Histography;* Bernadotte Everly Schmitt, ed., *Some Historians of Modern Europe . . . ;* and Samuel William Halperin, ed., *Some 20th Century Historians: Essays on Eminent Europeans* (Chicago: University of Chicago Press, c. 1937, c. 1942, and c. 1960, respectively) are studies of individual historians on both sides of the Atlantic.

4 See Dexter Perkins, John L. Snell, *et al., The Education of Historians in the United States* (New York: McGraw-Hill Book Co., 1962) — summarized in W. Stull Holt, "The Education of Historians in the United States," *The American Historical Review,* LXVIII (Jan. 1963), 402–406; John L. Snell, *History as a Career: To Undergraduates Choosing a Profession* (16 pages, obtainable on request from the American Historical Association, 400 A Street, S.E., Washington 3, D.C.); *College Teaching as a Career* (free on request from American Council on Education, 1785 Massachusetts Ave., N.W., Washington 5, D.C.).

In the United States such once hotly argued subjects as the Civil War, international relations, and reform movements have largely lost their power to divide; and closely knit "schools" or cliques of interpretation — characteristic of an immature stage in the development of any field of study — have largely disappeared. Exceptions to these generalizations serve only to buttress their over-all validity.

Among the many things still needed to bring about a more effective utilization of these advances in the historical profession are (1) the bridging of the chasm that still divides our 30,000 secondary school history teachers from college professors — except those of the "teachers' colleges," (2) the achievement of a greater appreciation of the nature and value of history by the general public, and (3) the encouragement of research in innumerable segments of the experience of the past that still await investigation. The American Historical Association is giving special attention to the first of these challenges by directing one of its major programs toward making new historical discoveries and interpretations more quickly available to the high school classroom.[5] The phenomenal success of such nonprofessional historical periodicals as *American Heritage* and the rapid spread of Civil War round tables and similar study groups offer substantial encouragement in regard to the second. This booklet is directed primarily to the third of these needs, but in a modest way it hopes to serve all three.

The achievements and needs of history as a field of study, however great, do not in themselves justify your devoting to it the time and effort necessary to attain some degree of proficiency. You still need to ask the question:

2. Why study history? Any of three possible responses should give you an adequate and reassuring answer. Together they should be irrefutable.

a. As literature. For at least twenty-four centuries written history has stood as a major literary form. Effectively presented, it has the ability to depict the unfolding of fateful events and to portray the rise or deterioration of character in a manner that ranks it with great novels and epic poetry. This function of history makes it incumbent on every historian, whether an ex-

---

[5] Arthur Bestor, *The Restoration of Learning* . . . (New York: Alfred A. Knopf, 1955), a restatement of his earlier *Educational Wastelands,* sets forth some widespread criticisms of the disposition of departments and colleges of pedagogy to overemphasize teaching techniques and nonintellectual activities of pupils at the expense of subject matter. The AHA has issued to date some fifty pamphlets, under the editorship of George Barr Carson, Jr., and Walter Rundell, Jr., with others to follow, summarizing recent interpretations of every major field of history. Many are important guides to the bibliography of their respective fields. Of general interest is Margareta Faissler, *Key to the Past: History Books for Pre-College Readers* (2d ed.; c. 1959), 77 pp. A list of pamphlets available, in the form of an order blank, is obtainable from the Service Center for Teachers of History, The American Historical Association, 400 A Street., S.E., Washington 3, D.C. Prices run from $0.50 to $0.75 per single copy, with discounts for purchases in quantity. Some one-half million have so far been distributed. Available on request from the AHA is its Committee on Teaching, *Preparation of Secondary-School History Teachers* (Washington [1962]), 14 pp. See also the twenty-four essays in William H. Cartwright and Richard L. Watson, Jr., eds., *Interpreting and Teaching American History* (Washington: 31st Yearbook of National Council of Social Studies, 1961), xvi, 431 pp.

For additional comments on preparation for a life of scholarship in History see Chapter 1, following.

perienced practitioner writing a book or the neophyte preparing a class paper, to cultivate a style worthy of his theme. Oral presentation carries comparable responsibilities.

   b. As vicarious experience. All thinking is based, consciously or unconsciously, upon recollections of past experience. Man's unique ability to incorporate into his personal experience that of other men and women, not only of his own time but of all previous generations, is a true second sight that sets him above other species and enables him better to understand the present in order to prepare himself to face the problems of the future. The philosopher George Santayana warned that "when experience is not retained, as among savages, infancy is perpetual. Those who cannot remember the past are condemned to repeat it." (*Reason in Common Sense,* "Flux and Constancy — Continuity Necessary to Progress.") And Woodrow Wilson declared (*Public Papers: College and State,* I, 255), "The worst possible enemy to society is the man who . . . is cut loose in his standards of judgment from the past; and universities which train men to use their minds without carefully establishing the connection of their thought with that of the past, are instruments of social destruction." No two events in our lives or in the course of history are ever exactly alike, but recurring patterns of resemblance often make it possible for us to act with the confidence that comes from the recognition of the familiar. In the 19th and 20th centuries the heavy emphasis of the German army upon systematic and realistic studies of military history in its training programs was an important factor in enabling it to win great initial victories, while its opponents were having to relearn from their costly mistakes. In the end, the mystical self-delusions that were allowed to creep in and pervert German civilian history contributed to that nation's ultimate defeat and humiliation. An historian is not a daydreamer in an ivory tower. Only a person who is cognizant of the past can be a truly "practical" man, one able to free his mind from contemporary illusions and misconceptions and to select the path of safety and progress. He should also be a moral person, finding in the lessons of history pragmatic proofs of a Golden Rule pointing toward individual human rights and responsible democracy as the goal posts of civilization.

   c. As professional training. Finally, the discipline of history offers training for useful and satisfying, although underpaid, employment.

   (1) Direct. The teaching of history at both the advanced and secondary levels is entering a period of indefinite expansion as a result of increasing enrollments and of a steadily growing appreciation of the role of historical knowledge. In World War II the armed forces of the United States came at last to a realization of their needs in this field and began to sponsor the most extensive program of historical studies that the world has yet seen. Civilian agencies of the federal government have shown some signs of following this lead; and some state and local governments are already well advanced. Many business corporations are recognizing the continuing applicability of their past operational experience both by opening their records freely to independent researchers and by employing trained scholars without attempting to influence their conclusions.

(2) *Indirect.* Cognate fields and professions have long known that historical study was indispensable to their own proficiency, and this seems certain to increase as historians broaden their subject matter and continue to improve the quality of their offerings. One of the nation's greatest jurists, Judge Learned Hand, sagely wrote to the president of the American Association of University Professors (*AAUP Bulletin,* Summer 1956, p. 264),

> I think that the prime purpose of "higher education" is to establish the right habit of thinking, by which I mean thinking that holds its conclusions open to revision and is ready to consider any new evidence that is apparently reliable. That habit I believe is better acquired by a wide acquaintance with history, letters, and the arts than by specialized but limited disciplines. . . . The main thing is what will be the student's temper of approach to his problems when he gets through.

Without history the social sciences are like trees without roots, literature and the arts are flowering plants torn loose from the soil that nourished them, and philosophy runs the danger of becoming verbal gymnastics. The natural sciences, too, take on deeper implications and a broader outlook when coupled with history, both specialized and general.

3. How to study history. Systematic study is more effective and, in the end, takes less time than desultory reading and last minute "cramming." Some helpful suggestions are:

(1) Prepare and conscientiously follow a planned schedule of two- or three-hour study periods throughout each week at times when you will be most alert and in a place free from distraction. Colleges expect at least two hours of study a week for each hour of semester credit.

(2) After getting acquainted with a book (including textbooks) by skimming through it in the manner suggested by the first paragraph of Chapter 3, below, and paragraph 1-c of Chapter 6, read the assigned pages or chapter — if you are reading an entire book — at fiction-reading speed in order to grasp the over-all theme and content.

(3) Then reread it more meticulously with an eye to factual details and, while doing so,

(4) Make a succinct outline in tabulated form of *not more than one page* for each assignment or chapter, which can be perused at a glance.

(5) In the margin of this outline make a checklist of the more important names, events (with dates), terms, and other factual items in the assignment or chapter.

(6) Repeat this process for your notes on each class lecture.

(7) Review your outlines and checklists at least once a week, being sure that you grasp the relationship between the facts and the larger patterns of interpretation suggested by your outlines. You need both sound structural materials and a good blueprint to build a satisfactory house.

(8) Reread those portions of your book or lecture notes which your review shows have become vague in your memory or understanding.

(9) Make out sample examination questions and after answering them, revise your answers to make them clearer, better organized, more comprehensive and interpretive, and, at the same time, briefer and more to the point. Any type of essay question ("discuss," "trace," "compare") should be answered — after you have considered it for a moment and prepared an abbreviated outline for your guidance — in a single topic (or thesis) sentence or two, followed by a logical, systematic development of the factual and interpretive proof of your thesis and its implications.[6]

There yet remains one further question:

4. Why study historical methodology? He who seeks to learn anything about the past will profit from a knowledge of the methods by which it is reconstructed for later use. It will be essential to him in one or both of the following ways:

a. Training. The preparation and presentation of a first-rate classroom report, term paper, or thesis can be a most satisfying experience. And, although to a beginner the prospect of seeing his writing in print is likely to be both exhilarating and a little frightening, the difficulties in the way of eventual publication in some form may not — if he has had the proper training — be so forbidding as they may at first seem. The topics awaiting your attention are endless in number, potentially fascinating to you and your readers, and varied enough to suit any inclination or taste. More than three hundred periodicals publish articles in the field of American history with some degree of frequency; and newspapers are receptive to interestingly written feature articles, especially in the rewarding field of local history. Where capable historians do not adequately fill such needs, other writers are likely to be drawn to fill the vacuum — with no small danger of spreading distorted and erroneous conceptions.[7]

b. Appreciation. Even though you may never publish a line, training in research methodology will be invaluable to you. Anyone who has learned something of the techniques by which a picture is painted or a musical score composed can have a greater appreciation of an art exhibit or concert than one who has not. In the same way, anyone can increase his appreciation of a work of history if he understands the manner in which its raw material has been mined and assayed. Furthermore, he will be equipped to check any questionable interpretations and to go more deeply into matters that particularly interest him.

---

[6] For a detailed treatment see Clifford Thomas Morgan and James Deese, *How to Study* (New York: McGraw-Hill Book Co., 1957), 130 pp. Illus. and Walter Pauk, *How to Study in College* (Boston: Houghton Mifflin Company, 1962), 132 pp. Illus.

[7] Donald Dean Parker and Bertha E. Josephson, *Local History: How to Gather It, Write It, and Publish It* (New York: Social Science Research Council, 1944), xiv, 186 pp., with appendices and bibliographies, and Philip D. Jordan, *The Nature and Practice of Local History* (Washington: Service Center for Teachers, American Historical Association, c. 1958), viii, 45 pp. contain useful suggestions.

In brief, research consists of six steps. You need (1) to select an appropriate topic, (2) to track down all relevant evidence, (3) to take notes on it, (4) to evaluate critically the evidence you have collected, (5) to arrange it into a true and meaningful pattern, and finally, (6) to present it in a manner that will command interest and communicate to your readers the fullest possible understanding of the subject.[8]

---

[8] Allan Nevins, *The Gateway to History* (New York: D. Appleton-Century Co., 1938; paperbound Doubleday-Anchor reprint, revised, 1962) is a stimulating introduction to history as a key to the comprehension of human affairs, which should be followed by Louis Reichenthal Gottschalk, *Understanding History* . . . (New York: Alfred A. Knopf, 1950). Jacques Barzun and Henry F. Graff, *The Modern Researcher* (New York: Harcourt, Brace & Co., c. 1957) offers wise observations in a readable form. Carl G. Gustavson, *A Preface to History* (New York, etc.: McGraw-Hill Book Co., 1955) and Herbert Joseph Muller, *The Uses of the Past* (Mentor Books; New York: New American Library, c. 1952) relate their discussions of the nature of history to major periods of historical development. Fritz Richard Stern, ed., *The Varieties of History from Voltaire to the Present* (New York: Meridian Books, 1956) and Hans Meyerhoff, ed., *The Philosophy of History in Our Time: An Anthology* (Garden City, N.Y.: Anchor Books, 1959) bring together evaluations of the discipline by leading historians. Richard H. Bauer, *The Study of History, with Helpful Suggestions for the Beginner* (Philadelphia: McKinley Publ. Co., c. 1948) is an excellent brief treatment in 36 pages, including bibliographies. Sherman Kent, *Writing History* (New York: F. S. Crofts & Co., 1941) offers much insight with a light touch. Samuel Eliot Morison, "Faith of a Historian," *The American Historical Review*, LVI (Jan. 1951), 261–75, contains the statement of basic precepts by a master practitioner. It is reprinted, with "History as a Literary Art" and other essays, in his *By Land and by Sea* . . . (New York: Alfred A. Knopf, 1953). For the study of American history in particular, Homer Carey Hockett, *The Critical Method in Historical Research and Writing* (New York: Macmillan Co., 1955) is an enlarged revision of his *Introduction to Research in American History,* which has been a standard treatise since 1931.

1 CHOICE OF A SUBJECT

> *Make no little plans; they have no magic to stir men's blood, and probably themselves will not be realized. Make big plans; aim high in hope and work, remembering that a noble, logical diagram once recorded will never die, but long after we are gone will be a living thing, asserting itself with ever growing insistency.*
>
> Daniel H. Burnham, Architect
> (biography by Charles Moore), II, 147.

> *The history of the world is the unfolding of human freedom.*
> Hegel, *Philosophy of History*, introduction.

In selecting a topic for research, you must first be certain that it meets *all four* of the following criteria:

1. Value. Your topic must be able to shed light on a significant, and in a sense universal, aspect of human experience — perhaps through your approaching it as a case study or by demonstrating its connection with some larger movement. Much depends on the treatment. The biography of an obscure person or the story of a small community takes on larger meaning when it is related to great events and evaluated as representative of far-reaching developments. On the other hand, genealogy and antiquarianism (the latter concerning itself solely with historical facts in themselves) are useful to the historian, but they are not history.

2. Originality. If your subject has been treated in some earlier investigation, you must be sure that you will be able to bring to it either (or both)

a. New evidence that is substantial and significant, or a

b. New interpretation of the evidence that is valid and demonstrable.

3. Practicality. Your undertaking must be trebly feasible in respect to:

a. Availability of sources to which you can have access without unreasonable inconvenience and with the assurance that you will be able to use them without the owner or repository attempting to censor your conclusions,

b. Your ability to make proper use of these sources through your previous background and training, including foreign languages and other technical prerequisites (see next page), and

c. Size. The scope of the topic you select must be suited to the medium in which you are presenting it (term paper, seminar report, article, thesis, dissertation, or book) and also to whatever deadline you may have to meet in the completion of your research. Most topics, however, can be expanded to take in a larger field or contracted to some constituent aspect after you have progressed sufficiently in your research to have a more accurate conception of the nature of your subject and the sources that bear upon it.

4. Unity. Every investigation must have a unifying theme, or be directed toward an integrating question or proposition, that offers you a point of departure, a direction of progression, and the promise of specific conclusions.

* * * * *

One's background for historical scholarship should, ideally, include:

a. **Practice in articulate and graceful expression,** written and oral (see Chapter VI), as emphasized in earlier American education and still stressed in the British system — lest the fruit of one's labors be despoiled by glib interlopers.

b. **Proficiency in reading and speaking one or more foreign languages,** through study and use of one such language from early elementary school — after which it should be relatively easy to become multilingual.

c. **Mastery of a secondary discipline** (such as art, economics, medicine, or natural science), combined with primary training in history (its sources, techniques, and interrelationships) to make one a specialist in the history of that field — more feasible as colleges are freed from having to devote much of the freshman and sophomore years to work for which the secondary schools should be responsible.

d. **Equipment for utilizing the insights of psychology** — see presidential address by Professor William H. Langer, "The Next Assignment," *The American Historical Review,* LXIII (Jan. 1958), 283–304, and, for an example of collaboration between historian and psychologist, Frederick Wyatt and William B. Willcox, "Sir Henry Clinton: A Psychological Exploration in History," *The William and Mary Quarterly,* 3d ser., XVI (Jan. 1959), 3–16 — taking care, as also in *c,* above, not to mistake a superficial vocabulary for usable knowledge.

e. **The imagination,** in a world now overwhelmingly industrial and urban, to comprehend a way of life until very recently predominantly rural — see Comer Vann Woodward, "The Populist Heritage and the Intellectual," pp. 141–66 in *The Burden of Southern History* (Baton Rouge: Louisiana State University Press, c. 1960), and Carl Bridenbaugh, "The Great Mutation," *The American Historical Review,* LXVIII (Jan. 1963), 315–31.

f. **A clear distinction between the vocation of history and an antiquarian hobby,** such as the current interest in Civil War battles — which many historians fear as a grown-up form of child's play tending to obscure the causes and consequences of that tragic holocaust (see Woodward, "Two Centennials: The American Civil War," *The Yale Review,* L (Summer 1961), 481–90, and

James I. Robertson, Jr., "The Civil War Centennial . . . ," *The American Archivist,* XXVI (Jan. 1963), 11–18.

    g. Broad culture — for which early home training is advantageous and lifetime application mandatory.

    h. Respect for the life of the scholar-teacher and dedication to its advancement in status and recompense to the forefront of the professions, in order that it may better serve the nation and the world.

2 PURSUIT OF EVIDENCE

There was once a recipe for rabbit stew, so it is related, that began with the sensible admonition, "First, catch your rabbit." The following references should serve to put you on the trail. From the bibliographies and footnote citations you will find in these works, from further clues contained in the works they cite, and from persistent inquiry and correspondence you should be able in the end to compile a working bibliography of all the known sources of information. You may even have the exciting experience of uncovering previously overlooked sources.

A. GENERAL

1. Library catalogues. Your first step will be to consult the card catalogue of your best available library or libraries. The cards, now generally obtained from the Library of Congress in multiple copies, are customarily filed by (1) *author* (surname first, with authors of the same name listed in order of their date of birth), (2) *title* (by first word except *a, an,* or *the,* or the equivalent in foreign languages), and (3) *subject,* under one or more headings, usually indicated at the bottom of the printed card. Keep in mind the fact that such prefixes as *de, da, van,* and *von* are not generally considered a true part of the surname of Continentals; that *Mc* is listed as though *Mac;* that Hispanic people commonly retain the mother's family name following the surname; that the order of names among Asians often varies from Occidental practice; that there is no completely standardized form of transliteration between different alphabets; and that the German umlaut "ö" and Scandinavian "ø" are equated with "oe," "ä" with "ae," and "ü" with "ue" in English. (See also Ch. 5, par. C-1-a, below.) You should prepare a checklist (which you will expand as your research proceeds) of key persons, places, periods, topics, and types of activities related to your subject and then see what your library lists for each one.[9] (Note that for ease in finding, it has been neces-

---

[9] For the most efficient use of any library consult Frank H. McCloskey, *The Library* (New York: Reader's Digest, 1945), 16 pp.; Merrill Thomas Eaton and C. M. Louttit, *A Handbook of Library Usage for Schools and Colleges* (Boston, etc.: Houghton Mifflin Co., c. 1935), 43 pp.; Leo E. LaMontagne, *American Library Classification, with Special Reference to the Library of Congress* (Hamden, Conn.: Shoe String Press, 1961), x, 433 pp.; Clara Beetle, *A. L. A. Cataloging Rules for Author and Title Entries* (2d ed.; Chicago: American Library Association, 1949), xxi, 265 pp.; Margaret Hutchins, Alice Sarah Johnson, and Margaret Stuart Williams, *Guide to the Use of Libraries: A Manual for College and University Students* (4th ed.; New York: H. W. Wilson Co., 1929), 245 pp.; *Ibid.* (abridged ed., rev.; 1936), 86 pp.; Ernest Albert Baker, ed., *The Uses of Libraries* (rev. ed.; London: University of London Press, 1930), viii, 338 pp.; Margaret Hutchins, *Introduction to Reference Work* (Chicago: American Library Association, 1944), xii, 214 pp., with bibliographical footnotes; and Jesse Hauk Shera, *Historians, Books, and Libraries: A Survey of Historical Scholarship in Relation to Library Resources, Organization, and Services* (Cleveland: Press of Western Reserve University 1953), xvi, 126 pp.; *Bibliographical Services throughout the World, 1950–1959.* UNESCO Bibliographical Handbook Series, No. 9, ed. Louise Noëlle Malclès, 228 pp.

sary, because of vagaries of library cataloguing, to list some items that follow in a form not in accord with that set forth in Chapter 5, Section C.)

You can often arrange to obtain the use of other books that are not in your own library through various interlibrary loan services about which your librarian will have information. Items held by the Library of Congress are listed, by author only (or, if anonymous, by first word of title), in

a. *A Catalog of Books Represented by Library of Congress Printed Cards Issued* [from August 1898] *to July 31, 1942.* 167 vols.; Ann Arbor, Mich.: Edwards Bros., 1942–46. With a 42 vol. *Supplement* through 1947, *ibid.*: J. W. Edwards, 1948. Continued as The [U. S.] *Library of Congress Author Catalog . . . 1948–1952.* 24 vols. (Vol. 24: *Films*); *ibid.*, 1953. Since continued as *The National Union Catalog: A Cumulative Author List . . . 1953–1957.* 28 vols. (Vol. 27: *Music and Phonorecords;* Vol. 28: *Motion Pictures and Filmstrips*); *ibid.*, 1958 — with monthly supplements cumulated quarterly, annually (all published by the Library of Congress), and quinquennially.

For listings by subject consult *The* [U. S.] *Library of Congress Catalog . . . Books: Subjects, 1950–1954.* 20 vols.; J. W. Edwards, 1955; and *. . . 1955–1959.* 22 vols.; Paterson, N. J.: Pageant Books, 1960. With quarterly supplements (published by the LC), cumulated annually (also by LC) and quinquennially. See also the Library of Congress publications, *Motion Pictures and Filmstrips,* quarterly, cumulated annually, and *Music and Phonorecords,* semiannual, cumulated annually. See further *Armed Forces Medical Library Catalog, 1950–1954.* 6 vols. (pt. 1: *Authors,* pt. 2: *Subjects*); J. W. Edwards, 1955. Continued in *National Library of Medicine Catalog, 1955–1959.* 6 vols. (pt. 1: *Authors,* pt. 2: *Subjects*); Washington: Judd & Detweiler, 1960. Also U. S. Army Medical Library, *A Catalogue of Incunabula and Manuscripts in the Army Medical Library,* by Dorothy M. Schullian and Francis E. Sommer. New York: H. Schuman for the Army Medical Library, [1948?]. xiii, 361 pp. Plates, facsims. Also *Library of Congress Catalog: Maps and Atlases,* published annually by the Library of Congress for 1953, 1954, and 1955, and thereafter included in *The National Union Catalog: A Cumulative Author List . . .* and *The Library of Congress Catalog . . . Books: Subjects* indicated above.

A number of libraries also maintain a

b. *Union catalogue* on cards to facilitate interlibrary lending. The largest of these, in the Library of Congress, covers some eight hundred American and foreign institutions. Entries from 1952 are published in *The National Union Catalog . . . 1952–1955: Imprints.* 30 vols.; J. W. Edwards, 1961, and since 1956 in *The National Union Catalog* of the above paragraph. There are some twenty other major ones, including those at Harvard and Brown universities, and in Philadelphia, Cleveland, Chicago, Nashville, Chapel Hill, Atlanta, Denver, Helena, and Seattle. Where it is not possible to borrow, you can often arrange by direct correspondence with the repository library to obtain microfilm or microprint copies at reasonable costs.

c. Hale, Richard Walden, Jr., ed., *Guide to Photocopied Historical Materials in the United States and Canada.* Ithaca, N.Y.: Cornell University Press for the American Historical Association, c. 1961. xxxiv, 241 pp. Bibl. Campion, Eleanor Este, *Union List of Microfilms.* Rev., enl., and cum. ed.; Ann Arbor, Mich.: J. W. Edwards, 1951. xvi pp., 1961 cols. With *Supplement, 1949–1952, ibid.,* 1953. vi pp., 995 cols. *Supplement, 1953–1955, ibid.,* 1957. 1019 cols. Also consult *Guide to Microforms in Print,* 1961–, ed. James Albert Diaz. Washington: Microcard Editions, Inc., 1961–. Annual publication planned. Helpful to the researcher is American Library Association, *Directory of Library Photoduplication Services in the United States, Canada, and Mexico.* 2d ed.; Chicago: University of Chicago Library. 1962. Includes some 800 libraries.

Also Ballou, Hubbard W., *Guide to Microreproduction Equipment*. 2d ed., rev.; Annapolis, Md.: National Microfilm Association, 1962. [viii] 519 pp. Illus. Annual Suppls. planned. *Educational Film Guide*, since 1936, and *Filmstrip Guide*, since 1948, are published and cumulated by the H. W. Wilson Co. of New York. See also Born, Lester Kruger, "Universal Guide to Catalogs of Manuscripts and Inventories of Archival Collections: A Proposal for Cooperative Listing," *College and Research Libraries*, XVII (July 1956), 322–29. Dr. Born, of the Library of Congress, under the auspices of the American Council of Learned Societies and supported by the Council on Library Resources, headed by Verner W. Clapp, has made a preliminary survey looking toward means of bringing about a world-wide cooperative microfilming of research materials.

Helpful also are the printed catalogues of foreign libraries, including

d. *Catalogue of Printed Books in the Library of the British Museum*. 95 vols.; London: William Clowes & Sons, Ltd., 1881–1900. With *Supplement*. 15 vols.; *ibid.*, 1900–1905. Lithoprint edition; 58 vols. and 10 vols.; Ann Arbor, Mich.: J. W. Edwards, Inc., 1946, 1950. New edition, *General Catalogue of Printed Books*. 51 vols. through DEZ; London: William Clowes & Sons, 1934–56. Remainder to be completed in photoprinted form by the British Museum about 1965–66 (Vol. 108, through HUL, published in 1962).

e. British Museum, Department of Printed Books, *Subject Index of the Modern Works Added to the Library . . . in the Years 1881–1900*. 3 vols.; London: The Trustees . . . . 1902. With quinquennial suppls. and preceded by Peddie, Robert Alexander, *Subject Index of Books Published up to and Including 1880*. 4 vols.; London: Grafton & Co., 1933–48. See also *The British National Bibliography*, 1950– . London: Council of the B. N. B., 1950– . Weekly, cumulated quarterly, annually, and, as *Cumulated Subject Catalogue*, quinquennially. Based on copyright deposits and arranged by Dewey decimal system. Indexed.

f. Wright, Charles Theodore Hagberg, and Christopher James Purnell, *Subject Index of the London Library, St. James Square*. 4 vols.: to 1909, 1909–22, 1923–38, 1938–53; London: William & Norgate, etc., 1909–55. See also London, the University of, *The Students' Guide to the Libraries of London . . .*, by Reginald Arthur Rye; 3d ed., rev. and enl.; London: University of London Press, 1928; xxv, 580 pp.; supplemented by Irwin, Raymond, ed., *The Libraries of London . . .* ; London: Library Association, 1949; iv. 234 pp.; and Harrod, Leonard Montague, *The Libraries of Greater London: A Guide;* London: Bell, 1951; vii, 252 pp.

g. Paris, Bibliothèque Nationale, *Catalogue générale des livres imprimés: Auteurs*. Paris: Imprimerie Nationale, 1897– . (Vol. 186, through THIRTY, publ. in 1960). Note here that volume numbers running to three or more digits may be given in Arabic numerals. See also UNESCO, *Répertoire des Bibliothèques de France*. 3 vols.; Paris: Bibliothèque Nationale, 1950–51.

h. Berlin Preussische Staatsbibliothek, *Berliner Titeldrücke Fünfjahrs Katalog, 1903–34*. 8 vols.; Berlin: Staatsbibliothek, 1935.

i. *Deutscher Gesamtkatalog der Preussischen Bibliotheken . . . .* Berlin: Preussische Druckerei- und Verlags-Aktiengesellschaft, 1931– . (Vol. 14, through BEET-HORDNUNG, published 1939.)

j. Esdaile, Arundell James Kennedy, and F. J. Hill, *National Libraries of the World: Their History, Administration, and Public Services*. 2d ed.; London: Library Association, 1957. xv, 413 pp.

k. Ash, Lee, *Subject Collections: A Guide to Special Book Collections and Subject Emphases as Reported by University, College, Public, and Special Libraries in the United States, the Territories, and Canada*. New York: R. R. Bowker Co., 1958. xiv, 476 pp.

l. Betts, Robert E., "The Resources of the Technical Libraries of Western Europe," *American Documentation,* X (Jan. 1959), 64–69.

Learn the subject classification system of your library so that you will know where the works which you will need are shelved; obtain, if possible, a stack permit to scan the shelves; and run through the card catalogue or shelf list, arranged by classification call number, to find titles of books that may be charged out. Unfortunately, the major classification systems (Dewey decimal, Library of Congress, and Cutter) were formulated at a time when the scope of history was thought of in a far too narrow fashion. As a result, a large proportion of books that properly belong under history are classified and shelved under other subjects.

2. Bibliographies.

a. The American Historical Association, *Guide to Historical Literature,* eds. George Frederick Howe, *et al.* New York: Macmillan Co., 1961. xxxv, 962 pp. Index. William Columbus Davis, central editor. Successor to *A Guide to Historical Literature,* eds. George Matthew Dutcher, *et al.* Macmillan Co., 1931. xxviii, 1,222 pp. Index.

b. Franz, Günther, ed., *Bücherkunde zur Weltgeschichte . . . .* Munich: R. Oldenbourg, 1956. xxiv, 544 pp.

c. Coulter, Edith Margaret, and Melanie Gerstenfeld, *Historical Bibliographies: A Systematic and Annotated Guide.* Berkeley: University of California Press, 1935. ii, 206 pp.

d. Reeves, Dorothea D., *Resources for the Study of Economic History: A Preliminary Guide to Pre-Twentieth Century Printed Material Located in Collections in Certain American and British Libraries.* Boston: Harvard Graduate School of Business Administration, 1961. viii, 62 pp.

e. *International Bibliography of Historical Sciences,* 1926– . Paris: Librairie Armand Colin for the International Committee of Historical Sciences, 1930. Annual. Represents resumption of *Jahresberichte der Geschichtswissenschaft . . . ,* 1878–1913. 36 vols.; Berlin: E. S. Mittler & Sohn, etc., 1880–1916. See also *Annual Bulletin of Historical Literature,* 1911– . London: Historical Association, 1912– .

f. American Universities Field Staff, *A Select Bibliography: Asia, Africa, Eastern Europe, Latin America.* New York: American Universities Field Staff, Inc., c. 1960. ix, 534 pp. Plus *Supplement, 1961.* 75 pp. Further supplemented by periodic *Reports,* with bibliographies, on various areas. Also U. S., Library of Congress, General Reference and Bibliography Division, *Current National Bibliographies,* comp. Helen Field Conover. Washington: Library of Congress, 1955. v, 132 pp. Also U. S., Library of Congress, General Reference and Bibliography Division, *Non-Self-Governing Areas with Special Emphasis on Mandates and Trusteeships: A Selected List of References,* comp. Helen Field Conover. 2 vols.; Washington: Library of Congress, 1947.

g. U. S., Library of Congress, General Reference and Bibliography Division, *A Guide to Bibliographical Tools for Research in Foreign Affairs,* comp. Helen Field Conover. 2d ed., with suppl.; Washington: Library of Congress, 1958. iii, 145 pp. Index. Also Langer, William Leonard, and Hamilton Fish Armstrong, eds. for period covering 1912–32, Robert Gale Woolbert, ed., 1932–42, and Henry L. Roberts, ed., 1942–52, *Foreign Affairs Bibliography.* 3 vols.; New York: Harper & Bros. for Council on Foreign Relations, 1933–55. Based on continuing bibliographical notes in quarterly issues of *Foreign Affairs.*

h. Myers, Denys Peter, *Manual of Collections of Treaties and of Collections Relating to Treaties*. Cambridge, Mass.: Harvard University Press, 1922. xlvii, 685 pp. Index. Also Aufricht, Hans, *Guide to League of Nations Publications: A Bibliographical Survey of the Work of the League, 1920–1947*. New York: Columbia University Press, 1951. xix, 682 pp. Index. And United Nations [Library], *Documents Index: United Nations and Specialized Agencies Documents and Publications*. Jan. 1950– . Monthly. *International Congresses and Conferences, 1840–1937: A Union List of Their Publications Available in Libraries of the United States and Canada*, ed. Winifred (Gregory) Gerould. New York: H. W. Wilson Co., 1938. 229 pp. International Committee for Social Sciences Documentation, *Études des bibliographies courantes des publications officielles nationales; guide sommaire et inventoire. A Study of Current Bibliographies of National Official Publications; Short Guide and Inventory*, ed. Jean Meyriat. Bibliographical Handbook No. 7. Paris: UNESCO, c. 1958. 260 pp. Also see U. S., Library of Congress, Division of Documents, *Government Document Bibliography in the United States and Elsewhere*. 3d ed.; Washington: Government Printing Office, 1942. 78 pp. And see *List of the Serial Publications of Foreign Governments, 1815–1931*, ed. Winifred (Gregory) Gerould. New York: H. W. Wilson Co., 1932. 720 pp. Note also *Public Availability of Diplomatic Archives in the United States and Foreign Countries*. Washington: Historical Office, Bureau of Public Affairs, Department of State, July 1961. 35 pp. Mimeographed.

i. *Bulletin of the Public Affairs Information Service*. New York: Public Affairs Information Service, 1915– . Published weekly, cumulated quarterly and annually.

j. Surrency, Erwin C., Benjamin Feld, and Joseph Crea, *A Guide to Legal Research*. 2d ed.; New York: Oceana Publications, 1959. 124 pp. Also Price, Miles Oscar, and Harry Bitner, *Effective Legal Research: A Practical Manual of Law Books and Their Use*. New York: Prentice-Hall, Inc., c. 1953. xii, 633 pp. Index.

k. Besterman, Theodore, *A World Bibliography of Bibliographies and Bibliographical Catalogues, Calendars, Abstracts, Digests, Indexes, and the Like*. 3d ed.; 4 vols.; Geneva: Societas Bibliographica, 1955–58. Also Malclès, Louise Noëlle, *Les sources du travail bibliographique*. 3 vols. in 4; Geneva: E. Droz, 1950–58.

l. Winchell, Constance Mabel, ed., *Guide to Reference Books*. 7th ed.; Chicago: American Library Association, 1951. xvii, 645 pp. Index. With triennial supplements. Formerly edited by Isadore G. Mudge. Semiannual suppls. in Jan. and July issues of *College and Research Libraries*. See also *The Bibliographic Index: A Cumulative Bibliography of Bibliographies, 1937– . New York: H. W. Wilson Co., 1938– . Annual, with cumulation at roughly five-year intervals.

m. *The American Historical Review*. Consult reviews of books and lists of articles in other periodicals in each quarterly issue of this magazine for items more recent than those covered by any of the above. Annual indexes (of book reviews and own articles) included; normally cumulated decennially. Most recent is *General Index for Volumes XLI–LX, 1935–1955*. New York: Macmillan Co., 1962. 431 pp. Other scholarly journals — for example *The American Neptune* for maritime history and *Isis* for the history of science — publish annual listings of books and articles pertaining to their special fields.

n. Fox, William Lloyd, *List of Doctoral Dissertations in History in Progress or Completed at Colleges and Universities in the United States since 1958*. Washington: American Historical Association, 1961. 61 pp. Appendix, pp. 60–61, by Patricia M. Fox, is a bibliography of previous editions of this *List* from 1905 through 1958 (*List . . . for 1947* — Washington: American Historical Association, 1947. 39 pp. — inadvertently omitted from Fox's Appendix. Every doctoral candidate, after having checked all previous lists, should *immediately* report the subject he has chosen for his dissertation, preferably on the official form which his departmental chairman should keep in stock, to the AHA, 400 A Street, S. E., Washington 3, D. C., to avoid conflict with a dissertation already under way. Discontinuance or change of subject ought to be reported with equal promptness.

o. *Dissertation Abstracts: Abstracts of Dissertations and Monographs in Microform.* Ann Arbor, Mich.: University Microfilms, Inc., 1961– . Monthly. Author and subject indexes cumulated annually. Continues *Dissertation Abstracts: A Guide to Dissertations and Monographs Available in Microform. Ibid.*, 1952–61. Annual. Which was a continuation of *Microfilm Abstracts: A Collection of Abstracts of Doctoral Dissertations and Monographs Available in Complete form on Microfilm*, 1938– 51, with varying subtitles, which absorbed *Doctoral Dissertations Accepted by American Universities, 1933–55.* New York: H. W. Wilson Co., 1934–56. Annual.

p. London, University, Institute of Historical Research, *Historical Research for University Degrees in the United Kingdom, 1931–32– .* (Bulletin of the Institute of Historical Research, Theses Supplements.) London, 1933– . Annual. *ASLIB Index to Theses Accepted for Higher Degrees in the Universities of Great Britain and Ireland, 1950– ,* ed. P. D. Record. London: Association of Special Libraries and Information Bureaux, 1954– . Ottawa, Canadian Bibliographic Centre, *Canadian Graduate Theses in the Humanities and Social Sciences, 1921–1946.* Ottawa: E. Cloutier, Printer to the King, 1951. 194 pp. Ottawa, National Library, *Canadian Theses: A List of Theses Accepted by Canadian Universities. Thèses canadienne,* 1952– . Ottawa, 1953– . Maire, Albert, *Répertoire alphabétique des thèses de doctorat ès lettres des universités françaises, 1810–1900* .... Paris: Alphonse Picard et Fils, 1903. vi, 226, i pp. Index. France, Ministère de l'Instruction Publique et des Beaux Arts, *Catalogue des thèses et écrits académiques, 1884/85– .* Paris, etc.: Hachette et Cie, etc., 1885– . Annual. Quinquennial cumulative index. *Bibliographischer Monatsbericht über neu Erschienene Schul- und Universitätsschriften (Dissertationen Programmabhandlungen, Habilitationsschriften, etc.)* 1889/90–1941. Leipzig: Gustav Fock Verlag, etc., 1890– 1942. Title varies slightly. Divided by subject. *Jahres-Verzeichniss der deutschen Hochschulschriften, 1885–1886– .* Berlin, etc.: W. de Gruyter, etc., 1886– . Title varies.

q. International Guides, *Quarterly Check-List of Oriental Studies.* Box 1141, Darien, Conn.: American Bibliographic Service, 1959– . Ancient, medieval, and modern.

r. *Paperbound Books in Print.* New York: R. R. Bowker Co., 1956– . Issued quarterly. Arranged by subject fields. *College Edition;* Spring, 1958– .

s. Brown, Everette Somerville, *Manual of Government Publications, United States and Foreign.* New York: Appleton-Century-Crofts, 1950. ix, 121 pp.

t. *External Research: A List of Studies Recently Completed* and *External Research: A List of Studies Currently in Progress.* Washington 25: Department of State, Office of Intelligence Research & Analysis, 1952– . Separate booklets cover some fourteen different areas. Also *International Politics*, monthly bibliography.

u. U. S., Department of Agriculture, *Bibliography of Agriculture,* July 1942– . Washington: Government Printing Office, 1942– . Monthly, with annual index. Also *World Agricultural Economics and Rural Sociology Abstracts.* Amsterdam: North Holland Publishing Co., 1959– . English, French, German, and Spanish editions. Quarterly, with annual index.

v. Reingold, Nathan, "Manuscript Resources for the History of Science and Technology in the Library of Congress," *Library of Congress Quarterly Journal,* XVII (May 1960), 161–69.

w. Record, P. D., *A Summary Catalogue of Western Manuscripts in the Bodleian Library at Oxford.* 7 vols. in 8; Oxford: Clarendon Press, 1895–1953.

x. *Répertoire bibliographique de l'histoire de France,* eds. Pierre Caron and

Henri Stein. 9 vols. planned; Paris: Auguste Picard, etc., 1923– . Also Molinier, Auguste Émile Louis Marie, *Les sources de l'histoire de France des origines jusqu'au 1815.* Paris: Alphonse Picard et Fils, 1901–35. Completed only to 1715.

y. Hunt, Robert Nigel Carew, *Books on Communism: A Bibliography.* London: Ampersand Ltd., c. 1959. x, 333 pp. Index. Annotated; includes U. K. and U. S. govt. publs.

3. Periodical indexes.

a. Scott, Franklin D., and Elaine Teigler, *Guide to the American Historical Review, 1895–1945: A Subject-Classified Explanatory Bibliography of the Articles, Notes and Suggestions, and Documents,* The American Historical Association, *Annual Report for the Year 1944,* Vol. I, pt. 2. Washington: Government Printing Office, 1945, pp. 65–292. Index. See also *AHR indexes* (2-m, above).

b. *Poole's Index to Periodical Literature, 1802–1881.* Rev. ed.; 2 vols.; Boston: Houghton Mifflin Co., 1891. With supplements for period from 1882 through 1906.

c. *Reader's Guide to Periodical Literature.* New York: H. W. Wilson Co., 1900– . Issued monthly, cumulated in annual volumes. Place of publication varies to 1913.

d. *International Index: A Guide to Periodical Literature in the Social Sciences and Humanities.* New York: H. W. Wilson Co., 1907– . To 1920 issued under title of *Reader's Guide Supplement.* Biennial. Triennial through 1958. Quarterly and annual supplements.

e. *Annual Magazine Subject-Index.* 42 vols.; Boston: F. W. Faxson Co., etc., 1908–49. Part II, from 1909, as *The Dramatic Index.*

f. *Union List of Serials in Libraries of the United States and Canada,* ed. Winifred (Gregory) Gerould. 2d ed.; New York: H. W. Wilson Co., 1943. 3,065 pp. With two supplements; 3d in preparation. Covers some 120,000 periodicals in 600 libraries. See also *New Series Titles, 1950–1960.* 2 vols.; Washington: Library of Congress, 1961. Continued monthly, with annual cumulations.

g. *British Union-Catalogue of Periodicals: A Record of the Periodicals of the World from the Seventeenth Century to the Present Day in British Libraries,* eds. James Douglas Stewart, Muriel E. Hammond, and Erwin Saenger. 4 vols. and suppl. to 1960; London: Butterworth Scientific Publications; New York: Academic Press, 1955–58, 1962.

h. Caron, Pierre, and Marc Jaryc, *World List of Historical Periodicals.* Oxford: International Committee of Historical Sciences; New York: H. W. Wilson Co., 1939. xiv, 391 pp. Also Boehm, Eric H., and Lalit Adolphus, *Historical Periodicals: An Annotated World List of Historical and Related Serial Publications.* Santa Barbara, Calif.: Clio Press, 1961. xviii, 618 pp.

i. *Historical Abstracts, 1775–1945: Bibliography of the World's Periodical Literature* (Summaries in English of articles), ed. Eric H. Boehm. Quarterly, 1955– . Annual index.

j. For various technical and special fields consult the following, paying particular attention to sections on "History," "Agricultural History," "Legal History," etc., as appropriate. *Agricultural Index,* 1916– (monthly, cumulated annually and triennially); *Applied Science and Technology Index,* 1958– (monthly, cumulated annually; successor to *Industrial Arts Index,* 1913–57); *Art Index,* 1929– (quarterly, cumulated annually and biennially); *Business Periodicals Index,* 1958– (monthly, cumulated annually; also successor to *Industrial Arts Index*); *Education Index,* 1929– (monthly, cumulated annually and biennially; covering U. S. and Great Britain); *Index to Legal Periodicals,* 1908– (monthly, cumulated semi-annually, annually, and triennially) — all published by the H. W. Wilson Co., New York. *Index to Foreign Legal Periodicals,* 1960– . London: Institute of Advanced Legal Studies, University of London, in cooperation with the American Association of Law Libraries, 1961– . Quarterly, cumulated annually, with decennial cumulation planned. Jones, Leonard Augustus, *Index to Legal Periodical Literature.* 3 vols.; Boston: Boston Book Company, 1888–1919. See also *Engineering Index,* 1884–1905. 4 vols. (I, 1884–91; II, 1892–95; III, 1896–1900; IV, 1901–1905); New York: Engineering Magazine, 1892–1906. Continued under same title, 1906– . Annual. Published by Engineering Magazine, 1907–19; American Society of Mechanical Engineers, 1920–34; and Engineering Index, Inc., 1934– , all of New York. Also *Quarterly Cumulative Index Medicus.* Chicago: American Medical Association, 1927– . Monthly supplements, semiannual cumulation. Successor to *Quarterly Cumulative Index to Medical Literature,* 1917–27, and earlier *Index Medicus,* 1879–1927. See also *Current List of Medical Literature.* Washington: Army Medical Library, 1941–49, weekly; 1950– , monthly.

4. Newspaper indexes.

These gain additional value from the fact that an index for one newspaper often serves to guide you to the approximate date when the topic was likely to have been treated in other newspapers, either through a one-time practice of widespread exchange among them or from the probability that they exhibited a simultaneous interest in the matter.

a. *Palmer's Index to "The Times" Newspaper,* 1790–1943. 601 vols.; London: Samuel Palmer, 1868–1943.

b. *The Official Index to The Times.* London: The Times, 1907– . Annual.

c. *The New York Times Index.* New York: New York Times Co., 1913– . Published monthly and cumulated quarterly through 1929, annually since that date. Indexes for Sept. 1851 through Sept. 1858, for 1860, and 1863 through June 1905 are on microfilm obtainable from the Photographic Service Division, New York Public Library for $32.

d. *New York Daily Tribune Index.* 30 vols.; New York: Tribune Associates, [1876–1907].

e. Brigham, Clarence Saunders, *History and Bibliography of American Newspapers, 1690–1820.* 2 vols.; Worcester, Mass.: American Antiquarian Society, 1947. Includes location of files of these newspapers. Also Brigham, "Additions and Corrections to History and Bibliography of American Newspapers, 1690–1820," in the American Antiquarian Society, *Proceedings,* LXXI (19 April 1961), 15–62.

f. *American Newspapers, 1821–1936: A Union List of Files Available in the United States and Canada,* ed. Winifred (Gregory) Gerould. New York: H. W. Wilson Co., 1937. xvi, 791 pp. The Library of Congress has, in typescript in the Newspaper Reading Room, a list of its own holdings, including microfilm copies, by states and cities.

g. Brayer, Herbert O., "Preliminary Guide to Indexed Newspapers in the United States, 1850–1900," *The Mississippi Valley Historical Review,* XXXIII (Sept. 1946), 237–58.

h. Schwegmann, George A., Jr., *Newspapers on Microfilm: A Union Check List.* 3d ed.; Washington: Library of Congress, 1957. 202 pp.

i. Merrill, John Calhoun, *A Handbook of the Foreign Press.* Baton Rouge: Louisiana State University Press, c. 1959. viii, 394 pp. Map.

5. Reference works and aids.

a. Langer, William Leonard, and Hans W. Gatzke, eds., *An Encyclopedia of World History, Ancient, Medieval, and Modern, Chronologically Arranged.* Rev. ed.; Boston: Houghton Mifflin Co., 1956. xi, 1,232, lxxxix pp. Maps, geneal. tables.

b. Larned, Josephus Nelson, ed., *The New Larned History for Ready Reference* . . . . 12 vols.; Springfield, Mass.: C. A. Nichols Pub. Co., 1922–24. Illus., maps, bibl. XII, 10,773–10,855.

c. *Encyclopaedia Britannica* . . . . For many historical purposes the 9th ed.; 25 vols.; 1875–89, and the 11th ed.; 29 vols.; 1911, are more helpful than the latest, 14th ed.; 24 vols.; 1929 with subsequent "continuous revision." See also *The Century Dictionary and Cyclopedia* . . . . Rev. and enl. ed.; 12 vols.; New York: Century Co., c. 1911. Illus., maps, charts.

d. Seligman, Edwin Robert Anderson, and Alvin Johnson, eds., *Encyclopaedia of the Social Sciences.* 15 vols.; New York: Macmillan Co., 1930–34. Also Zadrozny, John Thomas, *Dictionary of Social Science.* Washington: Public Affairs Press, 1959. viii, 367 pp.

e. Hastings, James, *et al.*, eds., *Encyclopaedia of Religion and Ethics.* 13 vols.; New York: Charles Scribner's Sons, 1908–26. Also *The Catholic Encyclopaedia* . . . . 16 vols., incl. index vol.; New York: D. Appleton Co., 1907–14. Supplements, 1921, 1954. To be replaced by *The New Catholic Encyclopaedia,* to be published in some 15 vols. by the Catholic University of America, about 1965.

f. *The Statesman's Yearbook.* New York, etc.: Macmillan Co., etc., 1864– . Also Mallory, Walter Hampton, *Political Handbook of the World: Parliaments, Parties, and Press* . . . . New York: Harper & Bros. for the Council on Foreign Relations, 1927– . Also *Keesing's Contemporary Archives: Weekly Diary of World Events.* Bristol, July 1931– . Also independently publ. in Amsterdam, Brussels, and Vienna. Useful for texts of official statements, etc.

g. Murray, James Augustus Henry, *et al.*, eds., *A New English Dictionary on Historical Principles.* 10 vols. in 13; Oxford: Clarendon Press, 1888–1928. Known generally as the "Oxford Dictionary." Also Onions, Charles Talbut, *et al.*, eds., *The Shorter Oxford English Dictionary on Historical Principles.* 3d ed., rev. with addenda; Oxford: Clarendon Press, 1959 (c. 1955). xxii, 2,515 pp. Such dictionaries assist you to acquire a broader and more exact vocabulary and to discover the particular meaning which a word may have had in a given period. See also Partridge, Eric, *Origins: A Short Etymological Dictionary of Modern English.* 2d ed.; London: Routledge & Paul; New York: Macmillan Co., 1958. xix, 970 pp.

h. Webster, Noah (original ed.), *Webster's Third New International Dictionary of the English Language.* Springfield, Mass.: G. & C. Merriam Co., 1961. cxxxii, 2,720 pp. Illus. However, in view of widespread criticism of this edition for failure to distinguish sufficiently between proper usage by people of education and culture and the vernacular of the quasi-literate, it is advisable also to consult the 2d edition, 1954 (cxxxii, 3,194 pp. Illus.), edited by the literary scholar, William Allan Neilson.

i. Neilson, William Allan, ed.-in-chief, *Webster's Biographical Dictionary* . . . . Springfield, Mass.: G. & C. Merriam Co., c. 1943. xxxvi, 1,697 pp. Also *Biography Index.* New York: H. W. Wilson Co., 1946– . Triennial, with quarterly supplement. And *Current Biography,* monthly. Indexed in preceding item. *Chambers' Biographical Dictionary,* ed. J. O. Thorne. Rev. ed.; Edinburgh: W. & R. Chambers, 1962. v, 1,432 pp.

j. Barnhart, Clarence L., and William D. Halsey, eds., *The New Century Cyclopedia of Names.* 3 vols.; New York: Appleton-Century-Crofts, Inc., c. 1954.

k. Grimal, Pierre, *Dictionnaire des biographies.* 2 vols. in 1. Paris: Presses Universitaires de France, 1958. Plates.

l. Keller, Helen Rex, *The Dictionary of Dates.* 2 vols.; New York: Macmillan Co., 1934. Also Steinberg, Sigfrid Henry, *Historical Tables, 58 B.C.–A.D. 1945* [i.e. 1955]. 4th ed.; London: Macmillan; New York: St. Martin's Press, 1956. x, 257 pp. And Dunan, Marcel, *Histoire universelle: Tableau général de l'humanité.* 2 vols.; Paris: Librairie Larousse, 1960.

m. Bartlett, John, *Familiar Quotations* . . . . 13th ed.; Boston: Little, **Brown &** Co., c. 1955. xxxiv, 1,614 pp. Also consult earlier editions.

n. *The Oxford Dictionary of Quotations.* 2d ed.; London, New York, etc.: Oxford University Press, 1953. xix, 1,003 pp.

o. Mencken, Henry Louis, *A New Dictionary of Quotations on Historical Principles* . . . . New York: A. A. Knopf, c. 1942. xiii, 1,347 pp.

p. *A London Bibliography of the Social Sciences* . . . . 4 vols.; London: London School of Economics and Political Science, 1931–32. With 5 suppl. vols., 1930–55, publ. to 1960. Also Samford, Clarence D., *Social Science Bibliography: Curriculum and Methodology.* Carbondale: Southern Illinois University Press, 1959. viii, 101 pp. Also Clarke, Jack Alden, *Research Materials in the Social Sciences.* Madison: University of Wisconsin Press, 1959. 42 pp. See also quarterly check-lists of Economics and Political Science, Ethnology and Sociology, Literary History, Musicology, Physics, etc., published since 1958 as part of International Guide series by the American Bibliographic Service, Darien, Conn.

q. Satow, Ernest Mason, and Neville Bland, *A Guide to Diplomatic Practice.* 4th ed.; London & New York: Longmans, Green & Co., c. 1957. 510 pp.

r. Faye, Helen, *Picture Sources: An Introductory List.* New York: Special Libraries Association, c. 1959. vii, 115 pp. Covers 389 collections in U. S., Canada, Latin America, and Europe. Also Vanderbilt, Paul, *Guide to the Special Collections of Prints and Photographs in the Library of Congress.* Washington: Government Printing Office, 1955. v, 200 pp. Index. See also Bruhn, Wolfgang, and Max Tilke, *A Pictorial History of Costume* . . . . New York: Frederick A. Praeger, c. 1955. 74 pp. Illus., 200 plates.

s. Sonnedecker, Glenn Allen, "Some Guidelines into the Historical Literature on Pharmacy," *The American Journal of Pharmaceutical Education,* XXIII (Spring 1959), 143–72.

6. Atlases and gazetteers.

a. Palmer, Robert R., *et al., Atlas of World History.* Chicago: Rand, McNally & Co., 1957. 216 pp., 128 maps (92 colored). Also Palmer, *Historical Atlas of the World. Ibid.,* c. 1961. 40 pp. Index. Paperbound.

b. Fox, Edward Whiting, and H. S. Deighton, *Atlas of European History.* New York: Oxford University Press, 1957. 64 maps; gazetteer, exercises. Paperbound.

c. Shepherd, William Robert, *Historical Atlas.* 8th ed.; New York: Barnes & Noble, 1956. 226 pp. maps, 115 pp. index.

d. Bartholomew, John George, *A Literary and Historical Atlas.* 4 vols.; London: J. M. Dent & Sons, Ltd.; New York: E. P. Dutton & Co., 1913–36.

e. Muir, Ramsay, *Historical Atlas, Mediaeval and Modern.* 8th ed.; London: George Philip & Son, Ltd., 1956. xvi, 31 pp., 96 colored maps.

f. *Atlas zur Weltgeschichte* . . . . Berlin, etc.: Georg Westermann Verlag Braunschweig, 1956. vi, 160 pp.

g. Zeissig, Hans, *Neuer Geschichts-und Kulturatlas* . . . . Hamburg: Atlantik-Verlag, c. 1950. 10 pp., 138 colored maps.

h. Breasted, James Henry, Carl F. Huth, and Samuel Bannister Harding, *European History Atlas.* 10th ed.; Chicago: Denoyer-Geppert Co., c. 1954. lxx, 62 pp. Paperbound.

i. *Hammond's Historical Atlas.* Maplewood, N. J.: C. S. Hammond & Co., 1957. 48 pp.

j. The Economist (London), *Oxford Economic Atlas of the World.* 2d ed.; Oxford: Oxford University Press, 1959. viii, 128, 152 pp. Paperbound, 128 pp. Also special vols. for particular regions.

k. Humlum, Johannes, *Atlas of Economic Geography.* 4th ed.; London: Meiklejohn & Son, Ltd., c. 1955. xii, 127 pp.

l. *Hammond's World Atlas For Students.* New York & Maplewood, N. J.: C. S. Hammond & Co., c. 1956. ii, 50 pp.

m. Bartholomew, John, ed., *The Times Atlas of the World.* 5 vols.; London: Times Publishing Co., 1955–59. Vol. I, *World, Australia, and East Asia;* II, *India, Middle East, and Russia;* III, *Northern Europe;* IV, *Mediterranean and Africa;* and V, *The Americas.*

n. Vidal de la Blache, Paul Marie Joseph, and L. Gallois, eds., *Géographie universelle.* 15 vols.; Paris: A. Colin, 1927–48.

o. *Rand McNally Cosmopolitan World Atlas.* New York, Chicago, & San Francisco: Rand McNally & Co., 1956. xxxii, 173 pp. Plates, index.

p. *Webster's Geographical Dictionary . . . ,* ed. E. E. Thompson. Rev. ed.; Springfield, Mass.: G. & C. Merriam Co., c. 1949. xxxi, 1,293 pp.

q. Seltzer, Leon E., ed., *The Columbia-Lippincott Gazetteer of the World.* 2d printing, with suppl.; New York: Columbia University Press; Philadelphia: J. B. Lippincott Co., 1962. 2,182 pp.

r. Boyd, Andrew Kirk Henry, and W. H. Bromage, *An Atlas of World Affairs.* 3d ed., rev.; New York: Frederick A. Praeger, 1962. 160 pp. Also paperbound.

s. Whyte, Fredrica Harriman, *Whyte's Atlas Guide.* New York: Scarecrow Press, 1961 . 172 pp.

t. Ristow, Walter William, *The Services and Collections of the Map Division, the Library of Congress.* Washington: Government Printing Office, 1951. 22 pp. Illus.

B. ANCIENT

1. Bibliographical references.

a. Delaporte, Louis Joseph, *Les Peuples de l'Orient méditerranéen: Le Proche-orient asiatique.* "CLIO": *Introduction aux études historique,* No. 1. 3d ed.; Paris: Presses Universitaires de France, 1948. xxxv, 361 pp. Index. Also Drioton, Étienne, and Jacques Vandier, *Id: L'Égypte.* 1952. xxxix, 676 pp. Also Cohen, Robert, *La Grèce et l'hellénisation du monde antique.* "CLIO," No. 2. 2d ed.; 1948. xlv, 695 pp. And Piganiol, André, *Histoire de Rome.* "CLIO," No. 3. 3d ed.; 1949. li, 612 pp.

b. Bury, John Bagnell, *et al.,* eds., *The Cambridge Ancient History.* 12 vols., 5 vols. of plates; Cambridge: Cambridge University Press; New York: Macmillan Co., 1923–39. Bibls. at ends of vols. New ed. being publ. in fascicles. Also Glotz, Gustave, *et al., Histoire générale.* 12 vols.; Paris: Presses Universitaires de France, 1925–47.

c. Swain, Joseph Ward, *The Ancient World.* 2 vols.; New York: Harper & Bros., c. 1950. Bibls. I, 553–68, II, 627–45.

d. Chambers, Mortimer, *Greek and Roman History.* Washington: American Historical Association Service Center for Teachers, c. 1958. 28 pp. Paperbound.

e. Greenidge, Abel Henry Jones, A. M. Clay, and E. W. Gray, *Sources for Roman History, 133–70 B. C.* Rev. ed.; New York: Oxford University Press; Oxford: Clarendon Press, 1960. viii, 318 pp.

f. Rounds, Dorothy, *Articles on Antiquity in Festschriften, an Index: The Ancient Near East, the Old Testament, Greece, Rome, Roman Law, Byzantium.* Cambridge, Mass.: Harvard University Press, 1962. 560 pp.

g. *International Guide to Classical Studies.* Annual, with quarterly checklist. Darien, Conn.: American Bibliographic Service, 1958.

2. Translated sources.

a. Smith, F. Seymour, *The Classics in Translation: An Annotated Guide . . . .* New York: Charles Scribner's Sons, 1930. 307 pp.

b. Loeb, James (founder), *Loeb Classical Library*. Cambridge, Mass.: Harvard University Press, 1912– . About 400 vols.

3. Aids and atlases.

a. Woodcock, Percival George, *Concise Dictionary of Ancient History*. New York: Philosophical Society, c. 1955. 465 pp. Also *The New Century Classical Handbook*, ed. Catherine B. Avery and Jotham Johnson, New York: Appleton-Century-Crofts, 1962. xiii, 1,162 pp.

b. Whibley, Leonard, *A Companion to Greek Studies*. 4th ed.; Cambridge: Cambridge University Press, 1931. xxxviii, 790 pp. Illus., maps.

c. Sandys, John Edwin, *A Companion to Latin Studies*. 3d ed.; Cambridge: Cambridge University Press, 1925. xxxv, 891 pp. Illus., maps.

d. Pauly, August Friedrich von, *Paulys Real-Encyclopädie der classischen Altertumswissenschaft*. Rev. by Georg Wissowa; Stuttgart: J. B. Metzler, 1894– . About 34 vols. published.

e. *Oxford Classical Dictionary*. Oxford: Clarendon Press, 1949. xix, 971 pp. Incl. bibls. Also *Oxford Bible Atlas*, ed. Herbert G. May. *ibid.*, 1962. 144 pp. Illus.

f. *Atlas of Ancient and Classical Geography*. New ed.; Everyman's Library; London: J. M. Dent & Sons, Ltd.; New York: E. P. Dutton & Co., c. 1933. xii, 268 pp.

g. Heyden, A. A. M. van der, and H. H. Scullard, *Atlas of the Classical World*. New York: Thomas Nelson & Sons, 1959. 221 pp.

h. Ullman, Berthold Louis, *Ancient Writing and Its Influence*. New York: Longmans, Green & Co., 1932. vii, 234 pp. Illus. Also Thompson, Edward Maunde, *An Introduction to Greek and Latin Paleography*. Oxford: Clarendon Press, 1912. xvi, 600 pp. Illus., bibl. Steffens, Franz, *Lateinische Paläographie* . . . . Berlin & Leipzig: W. de Gruyter & Co., 1929. xl, 125 pp.

i. Laurand, Louis, *Manuel des études grecque et latines*. New ed.; 2 vols.; Paris: A. & J. Picard, et Cie, 1955–57.

j. Seyffert, Oskar, Henry Nettleship, and John Edwin Sandys, *A Dictionary of Classical Antiquities: Mythology, Religion, Literature, Art*. Rev. ed.; New York: Meridian Books, c. 1956. vi, 716 pp. Indexes. Also Daremberg, Charles Victor, and Edmond Saglio, *Dictionnaire des antiquités grecques et romaines* . . . . 5 vols. in 10; Paris: Hachette et Cie, 1877–1929.

k. Nash, Ernest, *Pictorial Dictionary of Ancient Rome*. 2 vols.; New York: Frederick A. Praeger, c. 1961–62. Illus., plans.

C. MEDIEVAL

1. Guides and bibliographies.

a. Paetow, Louis John, *A Guide to the Study of Medieval History*. Rev. ed.; New York: F. S. Crofts & Co., 1931. xvii, 643 pp. Index.

b. Thompson, James Westfall, *Reference Studies in Medieval History*. 3d ed.; 3 vols.; Chicago: University of Chicago Press, c. 1925–30.

c. Williams, Harry Franklin, *An Index of Mediaeval Studies Published in Festschriften, 1865–1946* . . . . Berkeley: University of California Press, 1951. x, 165 pp.

d. Ricci, Seymour de, *Census of Medieval and Renaissance Manuscripts in the United States and Canada*. 3 vols.; New York: H. W. Wilson Co., 1935–40.

e. Case, Shirley Jackson, *et al.*, *A Bibliographical Guide to the History of Christianity*. Chicago: University of Chicago Press, c. 1931. xi, 265 pp.

f. Farrar, Clarissa Palmer, and Austin P. Evans, *Bibliography of English Translations from Medieval Sources*. New York: Columbia University Press, 1946. xiii, 534 pp.

g. Bonser, Wilfred, *An Anglo-Saxon and Celtic Bibliography, 450–1087, with*

Indices. 2 vols.; Berkeley: University of California Press; Oxford: Basil Blackwell, 1957. Also Hastings, Margaret, "High History or Hack History: England in the Later Middle Ages," *Speculum,* XXXVI (Apr. 1961), 225–53.

h. Halphen, Louis, and Y. Renourd, *Initiation aux Etudes d'Histoire du Moyen Age*. 3d ed.; Paris: Presses Universitaires de France, (c. 1940) 1952. 205 pp. Also Calmette, Joseph, *Le Monde féodal*. *"CLIO": Introduction aux études historiques,* No. 4. 3d ed.; *ibid.,* 1951. xlv, 479 pp. Index.

i. *International Guide to Medieval Studies,* annual, with *Quarterly Check-List of Medievalia*. Darien, Conn.: American Bibliographic Service, 1958.

j. Chevalier, Cyr Ulysse Joseph, *Répertoire des sources historiques du moyen âge*. New ed.; 2 vols. in 4; Paris: A. Picard et Fils, 1905–1907.

k. Potthast, August, *Bibliotheca Historica Medii Aevi . . . .* 2 vols.; Berlin: W. Weber, 1896. Reprinted 1955.

l. Atiya, Aziz Suryal, *The Crusade: Historiography and Bibliography*. Bloomington: Indiana University Press. 1962. 170 pp.

m. Lewis, Bernard, "The Muslim World," pp. 218–32 in AHA *Guide* (2-A-2-a, above).

n. *Speculum* and *The American Historical Review* for recent book reviews and articles.

2. Bibliographical references.

a. Gwatkin, Henry Melvill, *et al., Cambridge Medieval History*. 8 vols.; Cambridge: Cambridge University Press; New York: Macmillan Co., 1911–36. Planned by John Bagnell Bury.

b. LaMonte, John Life, *The World of the Middle Ages . . . .* New York: Appleton-Century-Crofts, c. 1949. Illus., maps, index. Bibl., pp. 766–82.

c. Clapham, John Harold, Eileen Power, *et al.,* eds., *Cambridge Economic History of Europe . . . .* 3 vols. to date; Cambridge: Cambridge University Press, 1941– .

d. *Progress of Medieval and Renaissance Studies in the United States of America and Canada*. Boulder: University of Colorado Press, 1923– . Title varies.

e. Ferguson, Wallace Klippert, *The Renaissance in Historical Thought: Five Centuries of Interpretation*. Boston: Houghton Mifflin Co., c. 1948. xiii, 429 pp. Bibl., 398–407; bibl. footnotes.

3. Manuscripts.

a. Clark, Kenneth Willis, *Checklist of Manuscripts in the Libraries of the Greek and Armenian Patriarchates in Jerusalem Microfilmed for the Library of Congress, 1949–50 . . . .* Washington: Library of Congress, 1953. 44 pp.

b. Clark, Kenneth Willis, *Checklist of Manuscripts in St. Catherine's Monastery, Mount Sinai, Microfilmed for the Library of Congress, 1950 . . . .* Washington: Library of Congress, 1952. 53 pp.

c. Kristeller, Paul Oskar, *Latin Manuscript Books before 1600: A List of the Printed Catalogues and Unpublished Inventories of Extant Collections*. New York: Fordham University Press, c. 1960. xxii, 234 pp.

d. Djapridze, David, *Mediaeval Slavic Manuscripts: A Bibliography of Printed Catalogues*. Cambridge, Mass.: Medieval Academy of America, 1957. xii, 134 pp.

4. Aids and atlases.

a. Roeder, William S., *Dictionary of European History*. New York: Philosophical Library, 1954. viii, 316 pp.

b. East, William Gordon, *An Historical Geography of Europe.* 4th ed.; London: Methuen & Co., c. 1950. xx, 480 pp.

c. Meer, Frederik van der, *Atlas of Western Civilization,* trans. T. A. Birrell. 2d ed.; Princeton, N. J.: D. VanNostrand Co., Inc., c. 1960. 240 pp. 53 maps in color, 966 illus.

d. Spruner, Karl von Merz, and Theodore Menke, *Hand-Atlas für die Geschichte des Mittelalters under neuen zeit.* 3d ed.; Gotha: J. Perthes, 1880. 42 pp.

e. McEvedy, Colin, and John Woodcock, *The Penguin Atlas of Medieval History.* Penguin Books, c. 1961. 96 pp.

f. Harvey, Paul, and J. E. Hasseltine, *The Oxford Companion to French Literature.* Oxford: Clarendon Press; New York: Oxford University Press, 1959. x, 771 pp. Maps.

g. Balteau, J., *et al.,* eds., *Dictionnaire de biographie française.* Paris: Librairie Lelouzey et Ané, 1933– . Vol. 50 to CONSTANTIN.

h. Johnson, Charles, and Hilary Jenkinson, *English Court Hand, A. D. 1066 to 1500.* Oxford: Clarendon Press, 1915. xlviii, 250 pp. Illus., bibl.

i. Boüard, Alain de, *Manuel de diplomatique française et pontificale.* 2 vols.; Paris: Auguste Picard, 1929–51. Supplements Giry, Arthur, *Manuel de diplomatique* . . . . New ed.; F. Alcan, 1925. xvi, 944 pp.

D. MODERN EUROPE

1. Bibliographies.

a. Calmette, Joseph Louis Antoine, *L'Élaboration du monde moderne.* "CLIO": *Introduction aux études historiques,* No. 5. 3d ed.; Paris: Presses Universitaires de France, 1949. xliv, 616 pp. Index. Also Sée, Henri Eugène, Armand Rébillon, and Edmond Préclin, *Le XVIIe siècle* . . . . "CLIO," No. 6. 3d ed.; c. 1949. xx, 525 pp. Also Préclin, Edmond, and Victor Lucien Tapie, *Le XVIIIe siècle.* "CLIO," No. 7. 2 vols.; 1952. Also Villat, Louis, *La Révolution et l'Empire (1789–1815).* "CLIO," No. 8. 3d ed.; 2 vols.; 1947. Droz, Jacques, Lucien Genet, and Jean Vidalenc, *Restaurations et révolutions (1815–1871).* Vol. I of *L'Époque contemporaine (1815– 1919).* "CLIO," No. 9. 1953. xvi, 660 pp. And Renouvin, Pierre, Edmond Préclin, and George Hardy, *La Paix armée et la Grande-Guerre (1871–1919).* Vol. II of *Id.* 2d ed.; 1947. xxviii, 708 pp.

b. Bromley, John Selwyn, and A. Goodwin, *A Select List of Works on Europe and Europe Overseas, 1715–1815.* Oxford: Clarendon Press, 1956. xii, 132 pp. And Bullock, Alan Louis Charles, and Alan John Percivale Taylor, *A Select List of Books on European History, 1815–1914.* 2d ed.; ibid., 1957. 79 pp.

c. Ragatz, Lowell Joseph, *A Bibliography for the Study of European History, 1815 to 1939.* Ann Arbor, Mich.: Edwards Bros., c. 1942. xiv, 272 pp. With three supplements: I, 1943, 74 pp.; II, 1945, 73 pp.; III, 1955, 154 pp. See also U. S., Library of Congress, European Affairs Division, *Introduction to Europe: A Selective Guide to Background Reading,* comp. Helen Field Conover. Washington: Library of Congress, 1950. 201 pp. *Supplement,* 1955. 181 pp.

d. Herre, Franz, and Hellmuth, Auerbach, *Bibliographie zur Zeitgeschichte und zum Zweiten Weltkrieg für die Jahre 1945–50.* Munich: Institut fur Zeitgeschichte, 1955. 254 pp.

e. Deutsch, Karl Wolfgang, *Interdisciplinary Bibliography on Nationalism.* Cambridge, Mass.: Technology Press of Massachusetts Institute of Technology, 1956. 165 pp. Also Pinson, Koppel Shub, *A Bibliographical Introduction to Nationalism.* New York: Columbia University Press, 1935. 70 pp.

f. Haussherr, Hans, *Wirtschaftsgeschichte der Neuzeit vom Ende des 14. bis zur*

Höhe des 19 Jahrhunderts. 3d rev. ed.; Köln-Graz: Böhlau Verlag, 1960. xv, 544 pp.

    g. Hopper, Vincent Foster, and Bernard D. N. Grebanier, *Bibliography of European Literature.* Brooklyn: Barron's Educational Series, c. 1954. 158 pp.

    h. Stieg, Louis F., *A Union List of Printed Collections of Source Materials on European History in New York State Libraries.* New York: New York Library Association, 1944. 112 pp.

    i. Gerould, Winifred (Gregory), *List of the Serial Publications of Foreign Governments, 1815–1931.* New York: H. W. Wilson Co., 1932. 720 pp.

    j. Stewart, John Hall, *France, 1715–1815: A Guide to Materials in Cleveland* . . . . Cleveland: Western Reserve University Press, 1942. xxxiii, 522 pp.

    k. Caron, Pierre, *Bibliographie des travaux publiés de 1866 à 1897 sur l'histoire de la France depuis 1789.* Paris: E. Cornély, 1907–12. xxxix, 831 pp.

    l. Farmer, Paul, *France Reviews Its Revolutionary Origins: Social Politics and Historical Opinion in the Third Republic.* New York: Columbia University Press, 1944. vi, 145 pp.

    m. Comité Français des Sciences Historiques, *Bibliographie annuelle de l'histoire de France du cinquième siècle à 1939.* Paris: Editions du Centre National de la Recherche Scientifique, 1955– . Annual.

    n. Gérin, Paul, *Bibliographie de l'histoire de Belgique, 1789–21 juillet 1831.* Louvain: Editions Nauwelaerts, 1960. 429 pp.

    o. Mitchell, Philip Marshall, *A Bibliography of English Imprints on Denmark through 1900.* Lawrence: University of Kansas Libraries, 1960. 85 pp.

    p. Bithell, Jethro, ed., *Germany: A Companion to German Studies.* 5th ed., rev. and enl.; London: Methuen & Co., c. 1955. xii, 578 pp.

    q. Gebhardt, Bruno, *Handbuch der deutschen Geschichte.* New ed. by Herbert Grundmann; 4 vols.; Stuttgart: Union Deutsche Verlagsgesellschaft, 1954–59.

    r. *Bibliographie der deutschen Bibliographien,* 1954– . Leipzig: Verlag für Buch- und Bibliothekswesen. Annual. Also *Bibliographie der deutschen Literatur.* Frankfurt am Main: V. Klostermann Wissenschaft, 1945– .

    s. *Jahresberichte für deutsche Geschichte,* 1949– . Berlin: Deutsche Akademie der Wissenschaften Verlag, 1952– . Supplemented for period from World War I by *Vierteljahrshefte für Zeitgeschichte.* Stuttgart: Deutsche Verlags-Anstalt, 1953– .

    t. Dahlmann, Friedrich Christoph, *Quellenkunde der deutschen Geschichte.* 2 vols.; Leipzig: K. F. Koehler, 1931–32. Often referred to as "Dahlmann-Waitz."

    u. "Bibliography of Finished and Unfinished Austrian and American Doctoral Dissertations on Austrian History," in University of Texas, Department of History, *Austrian History News Letter.* No. 1, 1960, *et seq.*

    v. *The Journal of Modern History* and *The American Historical Review* for recent book reviews, articles, and lists of articles.

    w. See also various catalogues of Stanford University Hoover Institute and Library . . . .

    x. Busse, Gisela von, *West German Library Developments since 1945, with Special Emphasis on the Rebuilding of Research Libraries.* Washington: Government Printing Office, 1962. vii, 82 pp.

    y. International Guides, *Quarterly Check-List of Renaissance Studies.* Darien, Conn.: American Bibliographic Service, 1959– .

    z. Sánchez Alonso, Benito, *Fuentes de la historia española e hispanoamericana* . . . . 3d ed.; 3 vols.; Madrid: Consejo Superior de Investigaciones Científicas, 1952.

2. Bibliographical references.

    a. *Histoire et historiens depuis cinquante ans . . . de 1876 à 1926* . . . . 2 vols.; Paris: F. Alcan, 1927–28. An introduction to historical studies by countries.

b. Ward, Adolphus William, *et al.*, eds., *The Cambridge Modern History.* 14 vols.; Cambridge: Cambridge University Press, 1902–1906. Bibls. at end of vols. "Genealogical Tables and Lists," XIII, 1–205. *Atlas, XIV.* 2d ed. regrettably lacks bibliography.

c. Langer, William Leonard, ed., *The Rise of Modern Europe.* 20 vols.; New York: Harper & Bros., 1934– . (13 vols. published to date).

d. *Peuples et civilisations,* eds. Louis Halphen and Philippe Sagnac. 20 vols.; Paris: F. Alcan, etc., 1926– .

e. Renouvin, Pierre, ed., *Histoire des relations internationales.* 7 vols.; Paris: Hachette et Cie, 1953– .

f. Taylor, Alan John Percivale, *The Struggle for Mastery in Europe, 1848–1918.* Oxford: Clarendon Press, 1954. See bibliographical essay, pp. 569–601.

g. Palmer, Robert Roswell, *A History of the Modern World.* New York: Alfred A. Knopf, 1950. Bibl. by Fredrick Aandahl, Jr., pp. 845–900.

h. Heaton, Herbert, *Economic History of Europe.* Rev. ed.; New York: Harper & Bros., c. 1948. xiv, 792 pp. Maps, charts, index.

i. Pinson, Koppel Shub, *Modern Germany* . . . . New York: Macmillan Co., 1954. Bibl. notes, pp. 579–613.

3. Manuscripts.

a. Thomas, Daniel H., and Lynn Marshall Case, *Guide to the Diplomatic Archives of Western Europe.* Philadelphia: University of Pennsylvania Press, c. 1959. xii, 389 pp.

b. France, Direction des Archives, *Catalogue des microfilms de sécurité et de complément conservés dans des départments,* by Michel Duchein. Paris: Imprimerie Nationale, 1955. 260 pp. *Ier supplément, 1955–58,* by Michel Duchein, Emmanuel Poulle, and Alexandre Labat. *Ibid.,* 1960. 410 pp.

c. The American Historical Association Committee for the Study of War Documents, *A Catalogue of Files and Microfilms of the German Foreign Ministry Archives, 1867–1920.* Oxford: Oxford University Press, c. 1959. xliv pp., 1,290 triple cols. Continued in U. S., Dept. of State, Historical Office, *A Catalog of Files and Microfilms of the German Foreign Ministry Archives, 1920–1945,* ed. George Otto Kent. 3 vols. planned; Stanford, Calif.: Hoover Institution, 1962– . Also Weinberg, Gerhard, and Fritz T. Epstein, *Guide to Captured German Documents.* Maxwell Air Force Base, Ala.: Air University Human Resources Research Institute, 1952. ix, 90 pp. Also Weinberg, *Supplement* . . . . Washington: National Archives, 1959. vi, 69 pp. See *Publications of the National Archives and Records Service* (Washington 25, D. C.: Mar. 1963. 10 pp. With frequent rev. eds. (obtainable on request), especially pp. 8–9, for lists of documents obtainable on microfilm. Also Germany (Federal Republic, 1949–), Bundesarchiv, *Das Bundesarchiv und seine Bestände,* eds. Friedrich Facius, Hans Booms, and Heinz Boberach. *Schriften des Bundesarchiv,* No. 10. Boppard am Rhein, Germany: Harald Boldt Verlag, 1961. xvi, 211 pp.

d. *Übersicht über die Bestände des Deutschen Zentralarchivs Potsdam.* Berlin: Rütten & Loening, 1957. 232 pp.

e. Beers, Henry Putney, *The French in North America: A Bibliographical Guide to French Archives, Reproductions, and Research Missions.* Baton Rouge: Louisiana State University Press, 1957. xi, 413 pp.

4. Aids and Atlases.

a. Pounds, Norman J. G., and Robert C. Kingsbury, *An Atlas of European Affairs.* New York: Frederick A. Praeger, forthcoming. Ca. 125 pp. 59 maps, tables. Paperbound.

(See also 2-C-4, above.)

E. BRITISH COMMONWEALTH

1. Guides and bibliographies.

a. Kitson Clark, George Sidney Robert, *Guide for Research Students Working on Historical Subjects.* Cambridge: Cambridge University Press, 1958. 55 pp. Binns, Norman E., *An Introduction to Historical Bibliography.* London: Association of Assistant Librarians, 1953. 370 pp.

b. Gross, Charles, *The Sources and Literature of English History from the Earliest Times to about 1485.* 2d ed.; London & New York: Longmans, Green & Co., 1915. xxiii, 820 pp. Index. Revision in progress by Edgar B. Graves under sponsorship of the American Historical Association. Read, Conyers, *Bibliography of British History: Tudor Period, 1485–1603.* 2d ed.; Oxford: Clarendon Press for the American Historical Association and the Royal Historical Society of Great Britain, 1959. xxviii, 624 pp. Index. Davies, Godfrey, *Bibliography of British History: Stuart Period, 1603–1714.* Oxford: Clarendon Press, 1928. x, 459 pp. Index. Revision in progress by Mary Frear Keeler under sponsorship of the American Historical Association. Pargellis, Stanley McCrory, and D. J. Medley, *Bibliography of British History: The Eighteenth Century, 1714–1789.* Oxford: Clarendon Press, 1951. xxvi, 642 pp. Bibliography for 1789–1851 being prepared by Ian R. Christie and A. J. Taylor; for 1855–1914 by H. J. Hanham.

c. Grose, Clyde Leclare, *A Select Bibliography of British History, 1660–1760.* Chicago: University of Chicago Press, c. 1939. xxv, 507 pp.

d. Morgan, William Thomas, *A Bibliography of British History (1700–1715)* . . . . 5 vols.; Bloomington: Indiana University Press, 1934–42.

e. Zagorin, Perez, "English History, 1558–1640: A Bibliographical Survey," *The American Historical Review,* LXVIII (Jan. 1963), 364–84. Opening footnote lists other recent bibliographical articles sponsored by the Conference on British Studies and edited by Elizabeth Chapin Furber.

f. Note bibliograhical references in Clark, George Norman, ed., *The Oxford History of England.* 14 vols.; Oxford: Clarendon Press; New York: Oxford University Press, 1934–61.

g. Hall, Hubert, *A Select Bibliography for the Study, Sources, and Literature of English Mediaeval Economic History.* London: P. S. King & Son, 1960. xiii, 350 pp. Williams, Judith Blow, *A Guide to the Printed Materials for English Social and Economic History, 1750–1850.* 2 vols.; New York: Columbia University Press, 1926.

h. Humphreys, Arthur Lee, *A Handbook to County Bibliography* . . . . London: Strangeways & Sons, 1917. x, 501 pp.

i. Gross, Charles, *A Bibliography of British Municipal History* . . . . New York: Longmans Green & Co., 1897. xxxiv, 461 pp. Index. Historical Association, London (Special Series, S2, rev.), Local History Committee, *English Local History Handlist.* Rev. ed.; London: Historical Association, 1952. 74 pp. *A Short Bibliography and List of Sources for the Study of Local History and Antiquities.* London: G. Philip, 1947. 55 pp.

j. Matthews, William, *British Autobiographies: An Annotated Bibliography of British Autobiographies Published or Written before 1951;* Berkeley: University of California Press, 1955; xiv, 367 pp.; and Matthews, *Canadian Diaries and Autobiographies; ibid.,* 1950; 130 pp. Subject index.

k. Hancock, P. D., *A Bibliography of Works Relating to Scotland, 1916–1950.* 2 vols.; Edinburgh: University Press; Chicago: Quadrangle Books, c. 1959–60. Supplement to Mitchell, Arthur, and C. G. Cash, *A Contribution to the Bibliography of Scottish Topography.* 2 vols.; Edinburgh: Scottish History Society, 1917.

l. O'Higgins, Paul, "A Select Bibliography of Irish Legal History," *The American Journal of Legal History*, IV (Apr. 1960), 173–80.

m. Ford, Percy, and G. Ford, *A Guide to Parliamentary Papers: What They Are and How to Find Them, How to Use Them.* Oxford: Basil Blackwell, 1955. xiii, 79 pp. Also Ford, *A Breviate of Parliamentary Papers, 1900–1916. Ibid.,* 1957. xlix, 470 pp. Plus *Id., 1917–1939. Ibid.,* 1951. xlviii, 571 pp. Great Britain, Parliament, House of Commons, *Catalogue of Parliamentary Reports and a Breviate of Their Contents, Arranged under Heads According to the Subjects, 1696–1834.* House of Commons, *Reports and Papers,* No. 626. [London: 1836.] viii, 220 pp. Great Britain, Parliament, House of Commons, *Catalogue of Papers Printed by Order of the House of Commons from the year 1731 to 1800 in the Custody of the Clerk of the Journals.* [London?] 1807. Facsimile reprint, London: H. M. Stationery Office, 1953. ix, 101 pp. *Parliamentary Papers: A General Index to the Sessional Papers* [known also as "Parliamentary Blue Books"] *Printed by Order of the House of Lords or Presented by Special Command (1801–1885).* 3 vols.; London: H. M. Stationery Office, 1860–86. King, Firm, Publishers, London, *Catalogue of Parliamentary Papers, 1801–1900, with a Few of Earlier Date.* London: P. S. King & Son, c. 1904. vii, 317 pp. The form of entry for this volume compared with the following companion volume should alert the student and scholar, in his finding and citation of published government documents, to the aberrations that sometimes overcome library cataloguers. Great Britain, Parliament, House of Commons, Library, *General Index to the Bills, Reports and Papers Printed by Order of the House of Commons and to the Reports and Papers Presented by Command, 1900 to 1948–49.* London: H. M. Stationery Office, 1960. viii, 893 pp. Ford, Percy, and G. Ford, *Select List of Parliamentary Papers, 1833–1899.* Oxford: Basil Blackwell, 1953. xxii, 165 pp. Also index volumes for *Accounts and Papers* (known as "Sessional Papers") — bills, committee and commission reports (including "Command Reports" — see Ch. 5, par. C-2-b, below), etc. — published by H. M. Stationery Office at the end of each session of Parliament. Includes "Blue Books," so-called from traditional binding, which are important reports, usually of commissions, of general interest. Page citations in the index volume of each session are those added by hand to sets in the Parliamentary library and may not be found elsewhere. They help, however, to indicate the relative location of a given item.

n. Adam, Margaret Isabella, John Ewing, and James Munro, *Guide to the Principal Parliamentary Papers Relating to the Dominions, 1812–1911.* Edinburgh, etc.: Oliver & Boyd, 1913. viii, 190 pp.

o. Rose, John Holland, Arthur Percival Newton, and Ernest Alford Benians, *Cambridge History of the British Empire.* 8 vols.; Cambridge: Cambridge University Press, 1929–59. Bibl. at end of each vol.

p. Trotter, Reginald George, *Canadian History: A Syllabus and Guide to Reading.* New and enl. ed.; Toronto: Macmillan Co., Ltd., 1934. xiv, 193 pp. Winks, Robin W., *Recent Trends and New Literature in Canadian History.* Washington: American Historical Association Service Center for Teachers, c. 1959. v, 56 pp. Watters, Reginald Eyre, *A Check List of Canadian Literature and Background Materials, 1628–1950.* Toronto: University of Toronto Press, 1959. xx, 789 pp. Tanghe, Raymond, *Bibliography of Canadian Bibliographies. Ibid.,* 1960. 206 pp. Boyle, Gertrude Mabel, and Marjorie Colbeck, *A Bibliography of Canadiana, First Supplement: Being Items in the Public Libraries of Toronto, Canada, Relating to the Early History and Development of Canada.* Toronto: Public Library, 1959. 333 pp. Harvard University, Graduate School of Business Administration, Baker Library, *Studies in Enterprise: A Selected Bibliography of American and Canadian Company Histories and Biographies of Businessmen,* comp. Lorna M. Daniells. Boston: Harvard Graduate School of Business Administration, 1957. xiv, 169 pp. Appdcs., index.

q. U. S., Library of Congress, Division of Bibliography, *The British Empire in*

Africa: A Selected List of References . . . , comp. Helen Field Conover. 4 vols.; Washington: Library of Congress, 1942–43.

r. U. S., Library of Congress, Division of Bibliography, *New Zealand: A Selected List of References,* comp. Helen Field Conover. Washington: Library of Congress, 1942. 68 pp. Ragatz, Lowell Joseph, "Facilities for Historical Research in Australia," *The Historian,* XXI (May 1959), 271–80. Social Science Research Council of Australia, *Bibliography of Research in the Social Sciences of Australia, 1954–1957.* [Canberra:] Social Science Research Council of Australia, 1958. 51 pp. Also *Id.,* . . . 1957–1960. *Ibid.,* 1961. 67 pp. Also *Australian Social Science Abstracts,* by the Australian National Research Council, 1946– . [Melbourne, etc.] Semiannual. Annual cumulative index.

s. Alman, Miriam, ed., *ASLIB Directory: A Guide to Sources of Information in Great Britain and Ireland.* 2 vols.; London: Association of Special Libraries and Information Bureaus, 1957. Hewitt, Arthur R., *Guide to Resources for Commonwealth Studies in London, Oxford, and Cambridge.* London: Athlone Press, University of London, for the Institute of Commonwealth Studies, 1957. viii, 219 pp.

t. Walford, Albert John, and Leonard Maslin Payne, *Guide to Reference Material.* London: Library Association, 1959. viii, 543 pp.

u. Esdaile, Arundell James Kennedy, and Roy Stokes, *A Student's Manual of Bibliography.* 3d rev. ed.; London: Allen & Unwin for the Library Association, 1954. 392 pp.

v. *English Books, 1475–1640: A Cross Index by STC Number and Partial List of Microfilms.* Ann Arbor, Mich.: University Microfilms, 1936– . Annual, with cumulation anticipated. See also *The British National Bibliography.* London: Council of the British National Bibliography, Ltd., British Museum, 1951– . Annual. Arranged by subjects. Also *The English Catalogue of Books . . . Issued in the United Kingdom of Great Britain and Ireland,* 1801– . London: Publishers Circle, Ltd., 1914. Now annual and cumulated quadrennially. By author, title, and key words of title. Also Low, Sampson, *Index to the English Catalogue of Books: Index of Subjects, 1837–1880.* 3 vols.; London: Sampson Low and Son, 1858–84.

2. Current publications.

a. Royal Historical Society, London, *Writings on British History* . . . 1934– , eds. Alexander Taylor Milne, etc. London: Jonathan Cape, 1937– . Annual.

b. Frewer, Louis Benson, *Bibliography of Historical Writings Published in Great Britain and the Empire, 1940–1945.* Oxford: Basil Blackwell, 1947. xx, 346 pp. Index. Lancaster, Joan Cadogan, *Bibliography of Historical Writings Issued in the United Kingdom, 1946–1956.* London: University of London Institute for Historical Research, 1957. xxii, 388 pp. Historical Association, *Annual Bulletin of Historical Literature,* 1911– . London: Hist. Assoc., 1912– .

c. Works dealing with British America published 1902, 1903, 1906–35, 1939–40 included in *Writings on American History* (see item 2-I-1-c), below).

d. *The English Historical Review, The Canadian Historical Review, Historical Studies of Australia and New Zealand,* and *The American Historical Review* for reviews of books and lists of articles published later than those included in any of the other bibliographical aids in this field.

3. Periodicals and newspapers.

a. *The Subject Index to Periodicals.* London: Library Association, 1919– .

b. Hewitt, Arthur R., *Union List of Commonwealth Newspapers in London, Oxford, and Cambridge.* London: Athlone Press of the University of London; New York: Oxford University Press, 1960. ix, 101 pp.

c. Indexes to *The Times* (see 2-A-4-a and 2-A-4-b, above).

d. *Public Opinion* (London): *A Weekly Journal Embodying the Opinions of the Press on All the Great Topics of the Day, Political and Social.* London: G. Nole, etc., 1861– . Subtitle varies. Until about World War I provides convenient lead to editorial opinions, unfortunately often failing to give date of quotation.

4. Manuscripts.

a. Galbraith, Vivian Hunter, *Introduction to the Use of the Public Records.* Oxford: Oxford University Press, c. 1952. 112 pp.

b. Hepworth, Philip, *Archives and Manuscripts in Libraries.* Pamphlet No. 18. London: Library Association, 1958. 30 pp.

c. Gilson, Julius Parnell, *A Student's Guide to the Manuscripts of the British Museum.* London: Society for Promoting Christian Knowledge; New York: Macmillan Co., 1920. v, 7–48 pp. British Museum, Department of Manuscripts, *The Catalogue of the Manuscript Collections* . . . , comp. Theodore Cressy Skeat. London: The Trustees . . . , 1951. 43 pp.

d. Crick, Bernard R., and Miriam Alman, *A Guide to Manuscripts Relating to America in Great Britain and Ireland.* New York: Oxford University Press for the British Association for American Studies, 1961. xxxvi, 667 pp.

e. Great Britain, H. M. Stationery Office, London, *Public Record Office Lists and Indexes.* Vols. 1–55; reprinted, revised, and supplemented. 16 East 46th St., New York 17; Kraus Reprint Corp.; P. O. Box 34773, Valduz, Liechenstein: Kraus Reprint Ltd., 1963– . *The British Public Record Office: History, Description, Record Groups, Finding Aids, and Materials for American History, with Special Reference to Virginia.* Richmond: Virginia State Library, 1960. 178 pp.

f. Born, Lester Kruger, *A Checklist of the Microfilms Prepared in England and Wales for the American Council of Learned Societies, 1941–1945.* Washington: Library of Congress, 1955. xvii, 179 pp.

g. Emmison, Frederick George, and Irvine Gray, *County Records.* Rev. ed.; London: Historical Association, c. 1961. 32 pp.

h. Van Kersen, Lionel William, "The National Register of Archives," *The American Archivist,* XXIII (July 1960), 319–37.

i. *Preliminary Inventory, Manuscript Group 28: Records of Post Confederation Corporate Bodies.* Ottawa: Public Archives of Canada, 1960. 38 pp.

5. Aids and atlases.

a. *Dictionary of National Biography,* eds. Leslie Stephen and Sidney Lee. Rev. ed.; 22 vols.; London: Smith, Elder & Co.; New York: Macmillan Co., 1908–1909. With decennial suppls. Also *The Dictionary of National Biography: The Concise Dictionary* . . . . 2 vols.; Oxford and New York: Oxford University Press, 1953–61. Pt. 1 to 1900; pt. 2, 1900–50.

b. *Who's Who* . . . . London: Allen & Unwin; New York: Macmillan Co., etc., 1849– . Annual volumes. With necrologies, *Who Was Who* . . . . Vol. I, 1897–1915; II, 1916–28; III, 1929–40; IV, 1941–50.

c. Haydn, Joseph Timothy, and Horace Ockerby, *The Book of Dignities* . . . . 3d. ed.; London: W. H. Allen Co., Ltd., 1894. xxviii, 1,170 pp. Index. Also Horn, David Bayne, *The British Diplomatic Representatives, 1689–1789.* 2d ed.; New York: Oxford University Press, 1961.

d. *The Annual Register of World Events,* 1758– . General index, 1758–1819. Also Whitaker, Joseph, *An Almanack,* 1868– . London: Whitaker, 1869– . Annual. Also Steinberg, Sigfrid Henry, *A Dictionary of British History.* New York: St. Martin's Press, forthcoming.

e. Temperley, Harold William Vazeille, and Lillian M. Penson, *A Century of*

Diplomatic Blue Books, 1814–1914. Cambridge: Cambridge University Press, 1938. xvi, 600 pp. Also Vogel, Robert, ed., *A Breviate of British Diplomatic Blue Books, 1919–1939.* Montreal: McGill University Press, 1963. 474 pp.

f. Munby, Alan Noel Latimer, *Cambridge College Libraries: Aids for Research Students.* Cambridge: W. Heffer & Sons, 1960. xv, 55 pp.

g. Emden, Alfred Brotherston, *A Biographical Register of the University of Oxford to A. D. 1500.* 3 vols.; New York: Oxford University Press, 1957–59.

h. Wilding, Norman W., and Philip Laundy, *An Encyclopaedia of Parliament.* London: Cassell; New York: Frederick A. Praeger, 1958. 705 pp. Bibl.

i. Lloyd, John Edward, and R. T. Jenkins, *The Dictionary of Welsh Biography down to 1940.* London: Honourable Society of Cymmrodorion, 1959. lvii, 1,157 pp.

j. Martin, Allan William, and P. Wardle, *Members of the Legislative Assembly of New South Wales, 1856–1901: Biographical Notes.* Canberra: Australian National University, 1959. xii, 249 pp.

k. Harvey, Paul, ed., *The Oxford Companion to English Literature.* 3d ed.; Oxford: Clarendon Press, 1946. viii, 931 pp. Also Barnhart, Clarence Lewis, and William D. Halsey, eds., *The New Century Handbook of English Literature.* New York: Appleton-Century-Crofts, 1956. vii, 1,167 pp.

l. *An Historical Geography of England before A. D. 1800.* Cambridge: Cambridge University Press, 1936. xii, 566 pp.

m. Kerr, Donald Gordon Grady, C. C. J. Bond, *et al.,* *A Historical Atlas of Canada.* Toronto & New York: Thomas Nelson & Sons, c. 1960. ix, 120 pp. Index. See also Burpee, Lawrence Johnstone, *An Historical Atlas of Canada.* Toronto & New York: Thomas Nelson & Sons, 1927. vii, 32, 48 pp., incl. 31 col. maps.

n. Cumberland, Kenneth Brailey, *Southwest Pacific: A Geography of Australia, New Zealand, and Their Pacific Island Neighbors.* London: Methuen & Co.; New York: McGraw-Hill, 1956. xviii, 365 pp. Illus., maps, tables.

o. Partridge, Eric, *A Dictionary of Slang and Unconventional English . . . .* 5th ed.; 2 vols.; London: Routledge & Paul; New York: Macmillan Co., c. 1961.

p. Smith, William George, *The Oxford Dictionary of English Proverbs.* 2d ed.; rev.; Oxford: Clarendon Press, 1948. xxxi, 740 pp. Also Apperson, George Latimer, *English Proverbs and Proverbial Phrases: A Historical Dictionary.* London & Toronto: J. M. Dent & Sons; New York: E. P. Dutton & Sons, c. 1929. ix, 721 pp.

q. Mitchell, B. R., and Phyllis Deane, *Abstract of British Historical Statistics.* Cambridge & New York: Cambridge University Press, 1962. 588 pp.

r. Great Britain, Stationery Office, *Published by H. M. S. O.: A Brief Guide to Official Publications.* London: HMSO, 1960. 58 pp.

s. Powicke, Frederick Maurice, and E. B. Fryde, *Handbook of British Chronology.* Royal Historical Society Guides and Handbooks, No. 2. 2d ed.; London: The Society, 1961. xxxviii, 565 pp.

F. SLAVIC EUROPE AND RUSSIA

1. Guides and bibliographies.

a. Morley, Charles, *Guide to Research in Russian History.* Syracuse, N. Y.: Syracuse University Press, c. 1951. xiii, 227 pp.

b. Byrnes, Robert Francis, and Joseph Backor, "Eastern Europe," pp. 257–353 in Am. Universities Field Staff, *Select Bibliography,* and pp. 39–46 in *Supplement, 1961* (see 2-A-2-f, above). Also Thomson, Samuel Harrison, "Eastern Europe," pp. 567–620, and Epstein, Fritz T., "Russia and the Soviet Union," pp. 621–45 in AHA *Guide* (2-A-2-a, above).

c. Kerner, Robert Joseph, *Slavic Europe: A Selected Bibliography in the Western European Languages . . . .* Cambridge, Mass.: Harvard University Press. 1918. 402 pp.

d. Grierson, Philip, *Books on Soviet Russia, 1917–1942: A Bibliography and a Guide to Reading.* London: Methuen & Co., c. 1943. iv, 354 pp. Horecky, Paul Louis, Robert V. Allen, *et al.,* eds., *Basic Russian Publications: An Annotated Bibliography on Russia and the Soviet Union.* Chicago: University of Chicago Press, c. 1962. xxvi, 313 pp.

e. U. S., Library of Congress, General Reference and Bibliographical Division, *Guide to Soviet Bibliographies: A Selected List of References,* comp. John Thomas Dorosh. Washington: Library of Congress, 1950. v, 158 pp.

f. U. S., Library of Congress, Division of Bibliography, *The Balkans . . . : A Selected List of References,* comp. Helen Field Conover. 5 vols.; Washington: Library of Congress, 1943.

g. Byrnes, Robert Francis, *Bibliography of American Publications on East Central Europe, 1945–1957.* Bloomington: Indiana University, c. 1958. xxx, 213 pp.

h. Dossick, Jesse John, *Doctoral Research on Russia and the Soviet Union.* New York: New York University Press, 1960. 248 pp.

i. Akademiia Nauk SSSR, Fundamental'naia Biblioteka Obshchestvennykh Nauk, *Istoriia SSSR: Ukazatel' sovetskoi literatury* [History of the USSR: Index of Soviet Writings] *za 1917–1925 gg.* 3 vols. planned; Moscow: Akademiia Nauk SSSR, 1956– . Vol. I covers Russian history to 1861. See also suppl. [*Prilozhenie*].

j. Harkins, William Edward, *Dictionary of Russian Literature.* New York: Philosophical Library, c. 1956. vi, 439 pp.

k. Ruggles, Melville J., and Vaclaw Motecky, *Russian and East European Publications in the Libraries of the United States.* New York: Columbia University Press, 1960. 396 pp.

l. Vakar, Nicholas P., *A Bibliographical Guide to Belorussia.* Russian Research Center, *Studies,* No. 22. Cambridge, Mass.: Harvard University Press, 1956. xii, 63 pp.

m. Pundeff, Marin, "Bulgarian Bibliography, 1942–1958," *The American Historical Review,* LXVI (Apr. 1961), 628–93.

n. New York Public Library, Slavonic Division, *Dictionary Catalogue of the Slavonic Collection.* 26 vols.; Boston: G. K. Hall, 1959.

o. Maichel, Karol, J. S. G. Simmons, and Jack Pooler, *Guide to Russian Reference Books.* 6 vols.; Stanford, Calif.: Hoover Institution . . . , 1962– .

2. Historiographies.

a. Mazour, Anatole Gregory, *Modern Russian Historiography.* 2d ed.; Princeton, N. J.: D. Van Nostrand Co., c. 1958. 260 pp. Illus.

b. *Ocherki istorii istoricheskoi nauki v SSSR* [Essays on the History of Historical Studies in the USSR]. 3 vols. planned; Moscow: Academy of Sciences, 1955– .

c. Black, Cyril Edwin, ed., *Rewriting Russian History.* New York: Frederick A. Praeger, 1956. 413 pp.

d. Doroshenko, Dmytro, *A Survey of Ukrainian Historiography.* New York: Ukrainian Academy of Arts and Sciences in the United States, Inc., 1957. 456 pp.

3. Current publications.

a. *The Slavonic and East European Review.* London, 1922– . Title varies.

b. *The American Slavic and East European Review.* 1942–61. Title changed in 1961 to *The Slavic Review.*

c. Shaw, Joseph Thomas, *The American Bibliography of Slavic and East European Studies.* Bloomington: Indiana University, annual vols. for 1956–59. Cont. as annual suppl. to *The Slavic Review,* above.

d. *Problems of Communism.* Washington: U. S. Information Agency, 1952– .

e. *Bibliografia sovetskoi bibliografii,* 1939, 1946– . Moscow, 1941– . Annual.

f. Library of Congress, *Monthly Index of Russian Accessions* and *East European Accession Index.*

g. Smits, Rudolf, *Serial Publications of the Soviet Union, 1919–1957: A Bibliographical Checklist.* Washington: Government Printing Office, 1958. ix, 459 pp.

4. Bibliographical references.

a. Pares, Bernard, *A History of Russia.* Rev. ed.; New York: Alfred A. Knopf, 1953. Bibl. by Eleanor Buist, pp. 583–611.

b. Vernadsky, George, and Cyril Edwin Black, *A History of Russia.* 8 vols. planned; New Haven, Conn.: Yale University Press; London: H. Melford, Oxford University Press, 1943– . Bibls. at ends of vols.

c. *The Cambridge History of Poland.* 2 vols.; Cambridge: Cambridge University Press, 1941–50. Vol. III, bibliography, in progress.

d. Carr, Edward Hallett, *A History of Soviet Russia.* 6 vols.; London: Macmillan Co., Ltd.; New York: St. Martin's Press, 1950–60. Bibl. III, 567–85; IV, 377–79.

e. Rubinchek, Leonid Selik, *A Digest of the Krasnyi Arkiv.* Cleveland: Public Library, 1947. Continued separately by Leona Eisele.

f. Institut zur Erforschung der USSR, *Biographic Directory of the USSR, Compiled by the Institute for the Study of the USSR, Munich, Germany,* gen. ed., Wladimir [i.e. Vladimir] S. Mertšalov. New York: Scarecrow Press, 1958. ix, 782 pp.;

g. *Russkii Biograficheskii Slovar'* [Russian Biographical Dictionary]. 25 vols.; St. Petersburg: Imperial Russian Historical Society, 1896–1918. Also available on microcards — Microcard Editions, Inc., 901 26th St., N. W., Washington 7, D. C. $97.00.

5. Aids.

a. Strakhovsky, Leonid Ivan, *A Handbook of Slavic Studies.* Cambridge, Mass.: Harvard University Press, 1949. xxi, 753 pp. Bibls.

b. Florinsky, Michael T., ed., *Encyclopedia of Russia and the Soviet Union.* New York: McGraw-Hill Book Co., 1961. 624 pp. Also Utechin, Sergej V., *Everyman's Concise Encyclopaedia of Russia.* London: J. M. Dent, 1961. xxvi, 623 pp. Also Rouček, Joseph Slabey, ed., *Slavonic Encyclopaedia.* New York: Philosophical Library, 1949. xi, 1,445 pp.

c. *Bol'shaia sovetskaia entsiklopediia* [Great Soviet Encyclopedia]. 65 vols.; Moscow, 1926–47. 2d ed.; 1949– .

d. Slusser, Robert M., and Jan F. Triska, *A Calendar of Soviet Treaties, 1917–1957.* Stanford, Calif.: Stanford University Press, 1959. xii, 530 pp. Bibl., 450–60.

e. Horecky, Paul Louis, *Libraries and Bibliographic Centers in the Soviet Union.* Slavic and East European Series, Vol. XVI. Bloomington: Indiana University Publications, c. 1959. xviii, 287 pp.

6. Atlases.

a. *Historical Atlas of the USSR.* 3 vols.; New York: C. S. Hammond & Co., 1950.

b. Goodall, George, *Soviet Union in Maps . . . .* London: George Philip & Son, Ltd.; Chicago: Denoyer-Geppert Co., 1954. In colors. 32 pp.

c. *Oxford Regional Economic Atlas: USSR.* New York: Oxford University Press, 1957. 142 pp. Paperbound.

d. Balzak, S. S., *et al.,* eds., *Economic Geography of the USSR.* New York: Macmillan Co., 1949. xiv, 620 pp. Maps.

e. Russia (1923–USSR), Glavnoe Upravelenie Geodezii i Kartografi, *Atlas Mira,* ed. I. M. Itenberg. Moscow: 1960. 64 [i.e. 373] pp. Chiefly colored maps, folded. Also Telberg, Vladimir G., *English Translation to Atlas Mira.* New York: Telberg Book Co., 1958. 87 pp.

G. NEAR EAST AND AFRICA

1. Guides and bibliographies.

a. Davison, Roderic Hollett, *The Near and Middle East: An Introduction to History and Bibliography.* Washington: American Historical Association Service Center for Teachers of History, c. 1959. 48 pp. Also Davison, "European Archives as a Source for Later Ottoman History," pp. 33–45 in *Report on Current Research on the Middle East, 1958.* Washington: Middle East Institute, 1958. And Davison, "Where Is the Middle East?" *Foreign Affairs,* XXXVIII (July 1960), 665–75.

b. Ettinghausen, Richard, ed., *A Selected and Annotated Bibliography of Books and Periodicals in Western Languages Dealing with the Near and Middle East with Special Emphasis on Medieval and Modern Times.* With supplement. Washington: Middle East Institute, 1954. viii, 137 pp. Also *A Selected Bibliography of Articles Dealing with the Middle East* [1939–58]. 3 vols.; Jerusalem: Economic Research Institute, Hebrew University, 1954–59.

c. Davison, Roderic Hollett, "The Middle East since 1450," pp. 362–82, and McKay, Vernon, "Africa," pp. 745–69 in AHA *Guide* (2-A-2-a, above). See also London, University, School of Oriental and African Studies, *Historical Writing on the Peoples of Asia.* London & New York: Oxford University Press, 1961–62. Vol. IV, *Historians of the Middle East,* eds. Bernard Lewis and P. M. Holt. xi, 519 pp. Index.

d. Bayne, Edward A., *et al.,* "Southwest Asia," pp. 148–91, and Cowan, Laing Gray, and Edwin S. Munger, "Africa," pp. 195–253 in Am. Universities Field Staff, *Select Bibliography,* and pp. 15–38 in *Supplement,* 1961 (2-A-2-f, above).

e. Weber, Shirley Howard, *Voyages and Travels in Greece, the Near East, and Adjacent Regions Made Previous to the Year 1801 . . . .* Princeton, N. J.: American School of Classical Studies, 1953. vii, 208 pp. Also Weber, *Voyages and Travels in the Near East Made during the XIX Century . . . . Ibid.,* 1952. x, 252 pp.

f. Birge, John Kingsley, *A Guide to Turkish Area Study.* Washington: American Council of Learned Societies, 1949. xii, 240 pp. Maps, geneal. tables. Supplement with Karal, Enver Ziya, "Historiography in Turkey Today," *Middle East Affairs,* X (Oct. 1959), 318–24. Also Shaw, Stanford J., "Archival Sources for Ottoman History: The Archives of Turkey," in The American Oriental Society, *Journal,* LXXX (Jan.–Mar. 1960), 1–12. Melzig, Herbert, *Bibliographie universelle de la Turquie nouvelle.* Istanbul: Ulkü Kitap Yurdu, 1944. 223 pp. Koray, Enver, *Türkiye Tarih Yayinlari Bibliyografyasi* [Bibliography of Publications on History in Turkey], *1729–1950.* Ankara: Millî Eğitim Basimevi, 1952. 548 pp.

g. Spuler, Bertold, and Ludwig Forrer, *Der Vordere Orient in islamischer Zeit.* Bern: A. Francke, 1954. 248 pp. Gabrieli, Giuseppe, *Manuale di bibliografia musulmana . . . .* Pt. 1; Rome: Tipografia dell' Unione editrice, 1916. 489 pp. Pfannmüller, Gustav, *Handbuch der Islam-Literatur.* Berlin & Leipzig: W. de Gruyter & Co., 1923. viii, 436 pp.

h. Thomsen, Peter, *Die Palästina-Literatur . . . .* 5 vols.; Leipzig: J. C. Hinrichs, 1911–37. Human Relations Area Files, Inc. (HRAF), *Handbooks and Annotated Bibliographies.* New Haven, Conn.: Human Relations Area Files, 1956– . On various Arab countries and Iran and Afghanistan.

i. *Palestine and Zionism: A Cumulative Author, Title, and Subject Index to Books, Pamphlets, and Periodicals.* 2 vols.; New York: Palestine Foundation Fund, 1946. Plus supplement for 1946–48.

j. Masson, Paul, *Eléments d'une bibliographie française de la Syrie* . . . . Paris: E. Champion, 1919. 528 pp.

k. U. S., Department of State, Library Division, *Point Four: Near East and Africa: A Selected Bibliography* . . . . Washington: Government Printing Office, 1951. ii, 136 pp.

l. Elwell-Sutton, Laurence Paul, *A Guide to Iranian Area Study.* Ann Arbor, Mich.: J. W. Edwards for the American Council of Learned Societies, 1952. 235 pp. Wilson, Arnold Talbot, *A Bibliography of Persia.* Oxford: Clarendon Press, 1930. x, 253 pp. Farman, Hafez Fitzhugh, *Iran: A Selected and Annotated Bibliography.* Washington: Library of Congress, 1951. ix, 100 pp.

m. Sauvaget, Jean, *Introduction a l'histoire de l'Orient musulman* . . . . Paris: Adrien-Maisonneuve, 1943. 202 pp.

n. Topping, Peter, "Greek Historical Writing on the Period 1453–1914," *The Journal of Modern History,* XXXIII (June 1961), 157–73.

o. *A Bibliography of African Bibliographies Covering Territories South of the Sahara.* 3d ed.; Cape Town: South African Public Library, 1955. 169 pp. U. S., Library of Congress, General Reference and Bibliography Division, *Africa South of the Sahara: A Selected, Annotated List of Writings, 1951–1956,* comp. Helen Field Conover. Washington: Library of Congress, 1957. vii, 269 pp. U. S., Library of Congress, Africana Section, *Africa South of the Sahara: An Introductory List of Bibliographies,* comp. Helen Field Conover. Washington: Library of Congress, 1961. 7 pp. U. S., Library of Congress, European Affairs Division, *Introduction to Africa: A Selective Guide to Background Reading,* comp. Helen Field Conover. Washington: University Press of Washington, c. 1952. ix, 237 pp. U. S., Library of Congress, Serial Division, *African Newspapers in Selected American Libraries.* 2d enl. ed.; Washington: Library of Congress, 1962. vii, 68 pp.

2. Bibliographical references.

a. Brockelmann, Carl, *History of the Islamic Peoples.* New York: G. P. Putnam's Sons, c. 1947. xx, 582 pp. Maps, bibl., pp. 539–49, index. Paperbound ed.

b. Lewis, Bernard, *The Arabs in History.* London & New York: Hutchinson's University Library, 1950. 196 pp. Maps, bibl., pp. 184–88, index. Also in Harper Torchbooks series, paperbound.

c. Gibb, Hamilton Alexander Rosskeen, *Mohammedanism: An Historical Survey.* 2d ed.; London & New York: Oxford University Press, 1953. ix, 206 pp. Bibl., pp. 192–200; index. Reprinted as a Galaxy Book.

d. Kirk, George Edward, *A Short History of the Middle East from the Rise of Islam to Modern Times.* 4th ed. rev.; London: Methuen & Co.; New York: Frederick A. Praeger, c. 1957. 308 pp. Maps, bibl., index.

e. Stavrianos, Leften Stavros, *The Balkans since 1453.* New York: Rinehart & Co., c. 1958. Bibl., pp. 873–946.

f. Wolff, Robert Lee, *The Balkans in Our Time.* Cambridge, Mass.: Harvard University Press, 1956. Bibl., pp. 588–96 and in footnotes.

g. Lenczowski, George, *The Middle East in World Affairs.* 3d ed.; Ithaca, N. Y.: Cornell University Press, c. 1962. Maps, bibl., pp. 688–709.

h. Lewis, Bernard, *The Emergence of Modern Turkey.* London & New York: Oxford University Press for Royal Institute of International Affairs, 1961. Bibl., pp. 481–95.

3. Current publications.

a. *The Middle East Journal* and *The American Historical Review* for reviews of books and lists of articles.

b. London, University, School of Oriental and African Studies, Library, *Index Islamicus, 1906–1955: A Catalogue of Articles on Islamic Subjects in Periodicals and Other Collective Publications,* comps. J. D. Pearson and Julia F. Ashton. Cambridge: W. Heffer, c. 1958. xxxvi, 897 pp.

c. U. S., Library of Congress, Africana Section, *Serials for African Studies,* comp. Helen Field Conover. Washington: Library of Congress, 1961. viii, 163 pp.

4. Aids and atlases.

a. *The Encyclopaedia of Islam* .... 4 vols. and suppl.; Leyden: Brill; London: Luzac & Co., 1913–38. Rev. ed. now appearing in fascicles. *Islam Ansiklopedisi.* Istanbul: Maarif Matbaasi, 1940–45; Millî Eğitim Basimevi, 1945–53; Maarif Basimevi, 1954– .

b. Pareja Casañas, Félix M., *Islamologia.* 2 vols.; Madrid: Editorial Razón y Fe, 1952–54.

c. Alderson, Anthony Dolphin, and Fahir Iz, *The Concise Oxford Turkish Dictionary.* Oxford: Clarendon Press, 1959. xii, 807 pp.

d. Ronart, Stephan, and Nandy Ronart, *Concise Encyclopaedia of Arabic Civilization: The Arab East.* Amsterdam: Djambatan; New York: Frederick A. Praeger, Inc., 1959. ix, 589 pp. Maps.

e. Fisher, William Bayne, *The Middle East: A Physical, Social, and Regional Geography.* 3d ed.; London: Methuen & Co.; New York: E. P. Dutton & Co., c. 1956. xiii, 522 pp. Maps, charts, diagrs., index.

f. Hazard, Harry W., *Atlas of Islamic History.* Princeton, N. J.: Princeton University Press, 1954. 49 pp.

g. Roolvink, Roelof, *et al., Historical Atlas of the Muslim Peoples.* Cambridge, Mass.: Harvard University Press, 1957. x, 40 pages of maps in color.

h. *Oxford Regional Economic Atlas: The Middle East and North Africa.* New York: Oxford University Press, 1960. 60 pages of maps in color.

i. Fage, J. D., *An Atlas of African History.* London: E. Arnold, 1958. 64 pp. 62 maps.

j. Horrabin, James Francis, *An Atlas of Africa.* 2d rev. ed.; New York: Frederick A. Praeger, Inc., 1961. 126 pp. 50 maps.

k. Boyd, Andrew, Patrick VanRensburg, and W. H. Bromage, *An Atlas of African Affairs.* New York: Frederick A. Praeger, 1961. 144 pp. 55 maps. Also paperbound. Also Pounds, Norman J. G., and Robert C. Kingsbury, *An Atlas of Middle Eastern Affairs.* New York: Frederick A. Praeger, forthcoming. Ca. 120 pp., 55 maps. Paperbound.

H. FAR EAST

1. General.

a. Nunn, G. Raymond, "Asia," pp. 3–191 in Am. Universities Field Staff, *Select Bibliography,* and pp. 3–14 in *Supplement, 1961* (2-A-2-f, above).

b. Pritchard, Earl H., *et al.,* "Early History of Asiatic Peoples," pp. 106–19, and "Asia since Early Times," pp. 233–361 in AHA *Guide* (2-A-2-a, above).

c. Kerner, Robert Joseph, *Northeastern Asia: A Selected Bibliography* .... 2 vols.; Berkeley: University of California Press, 1939. Covers China, Japan, and Asiatic Russia.

d. Quan, Lau-king, *Introduction to Asia: A Selective Guide to Background Reading.* Washington: Library of Congress, 1955. x, 214 pp.

e. Clyde, Paul Hibbert, *The Far East* .... 2d ed.; New York: Prentice-Hall, Inc., 1958. xxviii, 836 pp. Index. Bibl. at end of each chapter.

f. Stucki, Curtis W., *American Doctoral Dissertations on Asia, 1933–1958*. Ithaca, N. Y.: Cornell University Press, 1959. 131 pp.

g. Nunn, G. Raymond, and Tsuen-hsuin Tsien, "Far Eastern Resources in American Libraries," *Library Quarterly*, XXIX (Jan. 1959), 27–42.

h. London, University, School of Oriental and African Studies, *Historical Writing on the Peoples of Asia*. London & New York: Oxford University Press, 1961–62. Vol. I, *Historians of India, Pakistan, and Ceylon*, ed. Cyril Henry Philips. ix, 504 pp. Vol. II, *Historians of Southeast Asia*, ed. Daniel George Edward Hall. xiii, 342 pp. Vol. III, *Historians of China and Japan*, eds. William G. Beasley and Edwin George Pulleblank. viii, 351 pp.

i. London, University, School of Oriental and African Studies, *Handbook of Oriental History* . . . , ed. Cyril Henry Philips. (Guides and Handbooks, No. 6.) London: Royal Historical Society, 1951, viii 265 pp.

j. Sellman, Roger Raymond, *An Outline Atlas of Eastern History*. London: Edward Arnold, Ltd., c. 1954. 63 pp.

k. Müller, Friederich Max, ed., *The Sacred Books of the East*. 50 vols.; Oxford: Clarendon Press, 1879–1910.

l. New York Public Library, Reference Department, *Dictionary Catalogue of the Oriental Collection*. 16 vols.; Boston: G. K. Hall, 1960.

2. Current publications.

a. *Bulletin of Far Eastern Bibliography*, 1936–40. Washington: American Council of Learned Societies. Continued as part of

b. *The Far Eastern Quarterly*, 1941–46; and since 1946 issued as annual supplement. Enlarged in 1956 to become

c. *The Journal of Asian Studies*. With annual bibliographical supplement.

d. London, University, School of Oriental and African Studies, *Monthly List of Periodical Articles on the Far East and South East Asia*, May 1954– . Cumulated annually as *The Far East and South-East Asia: A Cumulated List of Periodical Articles*.

3. India.

a. Crane, Robert D., *The History of India: Its Study and Interpretation*. Washington: American Historical Association Service Center for Teachers of History, 1958. 46 pp. Also Chicago, University, College, *Introduction to the Civilization of India: Handbook* . . . . University of Chicago Press, c. 1961. 47 pp. Also Mahar, J. Michael, *India-Pakistan*. Tuscon: University of Arizona Press, forthcoming. 136 pp.

b. Wilson, Patrick, *South Asia: A Selected Bibliography on India, Pakistan, Ceylon*. American Institute of Pacific Relations, 1957. iii, 41 pp.

c. Wilson, Patrick, *Government and Politics of India and Pakistan, 1885–1955: A Bibliography of Works in Western Languages*. Berkeley: University of California, 1956. viii, 356 pp.

d. Morris, Morris David, and Burton Stein, "The Economic History of India: A Bibliographical Essay," *The Journal of Economic History*, XXI (June 1961), 179–207.

e. *Index to the Foreign and Political Department Records*, 1756– . New Delhi: National Archives of India, 1957– .

f. Rapson, Edward James, *et al.*, *Cambridge History of India*. 6 vols. planned — II (100–1100 A.D.) never published; Cambridge: Cambridge University Press, 1922–37. Bibls. at ends of vols. Suppl. vol., Wheeler, Mortimer, *The Indus Civilization*. 1953.

g. Majumdar, Ramesh Chandra, *et al.*, *An Advanced History of India*. 2d ed.; London: Macmillan Ltd., 1950. Bibl., pp. 265–72, 617–26, 1023–41.

h. Majumdar, Ramesh Chandra, ed., *The History and Culture of the Indian People*. 10 vols. planned; London: Allen & Unwin, 1951– . Bibls. at ends of vols.

i. Nilakanta-Sastri, Kallidaikurichi Aiyah Aiyar, and H. S. Ramanna, *Historical Method in Relation to Indian History*. Madras: S. Wiswanathan, 1956. 184 pp.

j. Dowson, John, *A Classical Dictionary of Hindu Mythology and Religion, Geography, History, and Literature*. 6th ed.; London: K. Paul, Trench, Trubner & Co., 1928. xix, 411 pp.

k. Poleman, Horace Irwin, *A Census of Indic Manuscripts in the United States and Canada*. New Haven, Conn.: American Oriental Society, 1938. xxix, 542 pp. Indexes.

l. Davies, Cuthbert Collin, *An Historical Atlas of the Indian Peninsula*. 2d ed.; New York: Oxford University Press, 1959. 94 pp. 47 maps.

m. Turner, R. Lister, *A Comparative Dictionary of the Indo-Aryan Languages*. New York: Oxford University Press, 1962. 80 pp. Paperbound.

4. Southeast Asia.

a. Hobbs, Cecil Carleton, *Southeast Asia: An Annotated Bibliography* . . . . Washington: Library of Congress, 1952. 163 pp.

b. Embree, John Fee, and Lillian Ota Dotson, *Bibliography of the Peoples and Cultures of Mainland Southeast Asia*. New Haven, Conn.: Yale University Press, 1950. xxxiii, 821 pp. Maps.

c. Kennedy, Raymond, *Bibliography of Indonesian Peoples and Cultures*. 2 vols.; New Haven, Conn.: Human Relations Area Files, 1955.

d. Hall, Daniel George Edward, *A History of South-East Asia*. New York: St. Martin's Press, c. 1955. Bibl., pp. 763–89.

e. Hackenberg, Robert, *Southeast Asia*. Tuscon: University of Arizona Press, forthcoming.

5. China.

a. Hucker, Charles O., *Chinese History: A Bibliographical Review*. Washington: American Historical Association Service Center for Teachers of History, 1958. 42 pp. Also Goodrich, Luther Carrington, and H. C. Fenn, *A Syllabus of the History of Chinese Civilization and Culture*. 6th ed.; New York: Bookman Associates, 1960. 59 pp. Also Hucker, *China: A Critical Bibliography*. Tuscon: University of Arizona Press, 1962. x, 125 pp.

b. Gardner, Charles Sidney, *A Union List of Selected Western Books on China in American Libraries*. 2d ed., rev. and enl.; Washington: American Council of Learned Societies, c. 1938. xi, 111 pp. Author index.

c. Cordier, Henri, *Bibliotheca sinica*. 5 vols.; Paris: E. Guilmoto, 1904–24. And Yüan, T'ung-li, *China in Western Literature: A Continuation of Cordier's Bibliotheca sinica*. New Haven, Conn.: Far Eastern Publications, Yale University Press, 1958. xix, 802 pp.

d. Yüan, T'ung-li, *Economic and Social Developments of Modern China: A Bibliography*. New Haven, Conn.: Human Resources Area Files, 1956. viii, 130, v, 87 pp. Fuerwerker, Albert, "Materials for the Study of the Economic History of Modern China," *The Journal of Economic History*, XXI (March 1961), 41–60.

e. Irick, Robert L., *American-Chinese Relations, 1784–1941: A Survey of Chinese Language Materials at Harvard*. Cambridge, Mass.: Harvard University Press, 1960. xxv, 296 pp.

f. Latourette, Kenneth Scott, *The Chinese: Their History and Culture*. 3d ed.; New York: Macmillan Co., 1946. xvi, 847 pp. Bibls. at ends of chapters.

g. Rostow, Walt Whitman, *et al.*, *The Prospects for Communist China*. Cambridge, Mass.: Technology Press of Massachusetts Institute of Technology; New York: John Wiley & Sons, Inc.; London: Chapman & Hall, Ltd., c. 1954. Bibl., pp. 327–74. Also Hsueh, Chun-tu, *The Chinese Communist Movement, 1921–1937: An Annotated Bibliography of Selected Materials in the Chinese Collection of the Hoover Institution on War, Revolution, and Peace.* Bibliographical Series No. 8. Stanford, Calif.: Hoover Institution, 1960. viii, 131 pp. Also Cole, Allan Burnett, *Forty Years of Chinese Communism: Selected Readings with Commentary.* Washington: AHA Service Center . . . , through New York: Macmillan Co., c. 1962. ii, 43 pp.

h. Gardner, Charles Sidney, *Chinese Traditional Historiography.* 2d ed.; Cambridge, Mass.: Harvard University Press, 1961. 120 pp.

i. Frankel, Hans Hermann, *Catalogue of Translations from the Chinese Dynastic Histories for the Period 220–960.* Berkeley: University of California Press, 1957. 195 pp.

j. Wang, Chung-min, and T'ung-li Yüan, *A Descriptive Catalogue of Rare Chinese Books in the Library of Congress.* 2 vols.; Washington: Library of Congress, 1958.

k. Yang, Lien-sheng, *Topics in Chinese History.* Cambridge, Mass.: Harvard University Press, 1950. vii, 57 pp. Bibls.

l. Hightower, James Robert, *Topics in Chinese Literature: Outlines and Bibliographies.* Rev. ed.; Cambridge, Mass.: Harvard University Press, 1953. ix, 141 pp.

m. Fairbank, John King, and Kwang-ching Liu, *Modern China: A Bibliographical Guide to Chinese Works, 1898–1937.* Cambridge, Mass.: Harvard University Press, 1950. xviii, 608 pp.

n. Têng, Ssǔ-Yü, and Knight Biggerstaff, *An Annotated Bibliography of Selected Chinese Works.* Rev. ed.; Cambridge, Mass.: Harvard University Press, 1950. x, 326 pp.

o. Herrmann, Albert, *Historical and Commercial Atlas of China.* Cambridge, Mass.: Harvard University Press, 1935. 112 pp.

6. Japan.

a. Hall, John Whitney, *Japanese History: A Guide to Japanese Reference and Research Materials.* Ann Arbor: University of Michigan Press, 1954. 165 pp. Also Hall, *Japanese History: New Dimensions of Approach and Understanding.* Washington: AHA Service Center . . . through New York: Macmillan Co., c. 1961. 63 pp.

b. Borton, Hugh, *et al., A Selected List of Books and Articles on Japan in English, French, and German.* 2d ed.; Cambridge, Mass.: Harvard University Press for the Harvard-Yenching Institute, 1954. xiv, 272 pp.

c. Uyehara, Cecil H., and Edwin G. Beal, *Checklist of Archives in the Japanese Ministry of Foreign Affairs, Tokyo, Japan, 1868–1945, Microfilmed for the Library of Congress, 1949–1951.* Washington: Library of Congress, 1954. xii, 262 pp.

d. Silberman, Bernard S., *Japan and Korea: A Critical Bibliography.* Tuscon: University of Arizona Press, 1962. xiv, 120 pp.

7. Pacific.

a. Taylor, Clyde Romer Hughes, *A Pacific Bibliography: Printed Matter Relating to the Native Peoples of Polynesia, Melanesia, and Micronesia.* Wellington, N. Z.: Polynesian Society, 1951. xxix, 492 pp. Index, map. U. S., Library of Congress, General Reference and Bibliography Division, *Islands of the Pacific: A Selected List of References,* comp. Helen Field Conover. Washington: Library of Congress, 1943, reissued 1945. 154 pp.

b. Houston, Charles Orville, *An Annotated Preliminary Bibliography of Philippine Bibliographies.* Manila: University of Manila, 1960. 69 pp.

c. Welsh, Doris Varner, *A Catalogue of Printed Materials Relating to the*

Philippine Islands, 1519–1900, in the Newberry Library. Chicago: Newberry Library, 1959. viii, 179 pp. Also Lietz, Paul S., *Calendar of Philippine Documents in the Ayer Collection of the Newberry Library. Ibid.,* 1956. xvi, 259 pp. Fiji, Central Archives, *Records of the . . . Government . . . June 1871–September 1875,* by S. Tuinaceya; and *Id., Records of the Land Titles Commission, Roturna, 1882–1883. Preliminary Inventory,* Nos. 1, 2. Sura, Fiji, 1960, 1961. Unpaged.

1. UNITED STATES

1. Bibliographies.

a. Handlin, Oscar, *et al., Harvard Guide to American History.* Cambridge, Mass.: Belknap Press of Harvard University Press, 1954. xxiv, 689 pp. Detailed bibliographies, mostly unannotated; bibliographies in special fields, pp. 106–108; for government documents, pp. 112–49. Unusually full index, pp. 547–689. Successor to the still somewhat useful Channing, Edward, Albert Bushnell Hart, and Frederick Jackson Turner, *Guide to the Study and Reading of American History.* Rev. and augm. ed.; Boston & London: Ginn & Co., 1912. xvi, 650 pp.

b. Beers, Henry Putney, *Bibliographies in American History: Guide to Materials for Research.* New York: H. W. Wilson Co., 1942. xv, 487 pp. Reprinted; Paterson, N. J.: Pageant Books, Inc., 1959.

c. *Writings on American History,* 1902, 1903, 1906–40, 1948– .

(1) Richardson, Ernest Cushing, and Anson Ely Morse, *Writings on American History, 1902.* Princeton, N. J.: Library Book Store, 1904. xxi, 294 pp.

(2) McLaughlin, Andrew Cunningham, *et al., Writings on American History, 1903.* Washington: Carnegie Institution, 1905. xiv, 172 pp.

(3) Griffin, Grace Gardner, *Writings . . . ,* 1906 through 1940. Annual volumes, 1906–36, biennial 1937–40. Volumes for 1906–1908 published New York: Macmillan Co., 1908–10; 1909–11, Washington: Government Printing Office, 1911–13; 1912–17, New Haven, Conn.: Yale University Press, 1914–19; 1918–40 published as supplementary volumes of the American Historical Association, *Annual Report* for appropriate years. Volumes through 1935 also cover British America and Latin America; volume for 1939–40 covers British America. Cumulative *Index to the Writings on American History, 1902–1940.* Washington: American Historical Association, 1956. vii, 1,115 pp. Made possible by the bequest of David Maydole Matteson and prepared for publication by William Columbus Davis. Plans are under way for a selective list to fill the gaps for 1904–1905 and 1941–47.

(4) Masterson, James E., *Writings . . . ,* 1948– , continued as supplementary volumes of the A. H. A., *Annual Report.* For the gap referred to above and since the most recent Masterson volume consult book reviews and lists of articles in *The American Historical Review.*

d. U. S., Library of Congress, General Reference and Bibliographical Division, *A Guide to the Study of the United States of America: Representative Books Reflecting the Development of American Life and Thought,* comps. Donald Harold Mugridge, Blanche Prichard McCrum, and Roy Prentice Basler. Washington: Government Printing Office, 1960. xv, 1,193 pp. The New York Public Library, Reference Department, *Dictionary Catalogue of the History of the Americas Collection.* 28 vols.; Boston: G. K. Hall, 1961. Also Carman, Harry James, and Arthur Webster Thompson, *A Guide to the Principal Sources for American Civilization, 1800–1900, in the City of New York: Printed Materials.* New York: Columbia University Press, 1962. xlvi, 630 pp. Index.

e. Bemis, Samuel Flagg, and Grace Gardner Griffin, *Guide to the Diplomatic*

History of the United States, 1775–1921. Washington: Government Printing Office, 1935. xvii, 979 pp. Index. Reprinted; New York: Peter Smith, 1951.

f. Albion, Robert Greenhalgh, *Maritime and Naval History: An Annotated Bibliography.* Rev. ed.; Mystic, Conn.: Maritime Historical Association, 1955. v, 93 pp. See also *United States Naval History, Naval Biography, Naval Strategy, and Tactics: A Selected and Annotated Bibliography.* 2d ed.; Washington 25, D. C.: Naval History Division, Office of the Chief of Naval Operations, Navy Department, 1959. v, 26 pp.

g. Larson, Henrietta Melia, *Guide to Business History* . . . . Cambridge, Mass.: Harvard University Press, 1948. xxvi, 1,181 pp. Also Harvard University, Graduate School of Business Administration, Baker Library, *Studies in Enterprise: A Selected Bibliography of American and Canadian Company Histories and Biographies of Businessmen,* comp. Lorna M. Daniells. Boston: Harvard Graduate School of Business Administration, 1957. xiv, 169 pp. Appdcs., index. Stroud, Gene S., and Gilbert E. Donahue, *Labor History in the United States: A General Bibliography.* Urbana: University of Illinois Institute of Labor and Industrial Relations, 1961. 167 pp. Index.

h. Burr, Nelson Rollin, *A Critical Bibliography of Religion in America.* 2 vols.; Vol. IV of *Religion in American Life,* eds. James Ward Smith and A. Leland Jamison. Princeton, N. J.: Princeton University Press, 1961. Illus., notes, indexes. See also Ellis, John Tracy, *A Guide to American Catholic History.* Milwaukee: Bruce Publishing Co., c. 1959. viii, 147 pp. Index.

i. Matthews, William, and Roy Harvey Pearce, *American Diaries . . . Written Prior to the Year 1861.* Berkeley and Los Angeles: University of California Press, 1945. xiv, 383 pp. Also Kaplan, Louis, *et al., A Bibliography of American Autobiographies.* Madison: University of Wisconsin Press, 1961. xii, 372 pp. Index. 6,377 entries.

j. Swem, Earl Gregg, *Virginia Historical Index.* 2 vols.; Roanoke, Va.: Stone Printing & Mfg. Co., 1934–36. Also Easterby, James Harold, *Guide to . . . South Carolina History* . . . . 2 pts.; Columbia: Historic Commission of South Carolina, 1949–50 [i. e., 1953]. Wilkinson, Norman B., S. K. Stevens, and Donald H. Kent, *Bibliography of Pennsylvania History.* Rev. ed.; Harrisburg: Pennsylvania State Bureau of Publications, 1957. xxx, 826 pp. Index. Thornton, Mary Lindsay, *A Bibliography of North Carolina, 1589–1956.* Chapel Hill: University of North Carolina Press, 1958. viii, 597 pp. Index. Streeter, Thomas Winthrop, *Bibliography of Texas, 1795–1845.* 5 vols.; Cambridge, Mass.: Harvard University Press, 1955–60. Blegen, Theodore Christian, and Theodore L. Nydahl, *Minnesota History: A Guide to Reading and Study.* Minneapolis: University of Minnesota Press, c. 1960. x, 223 pp. Maps. Shetler, Charles, *Guide to the Study of West Virginia History.* Morgantown: West Virginia University Library, 1960. vii, 151 pp. Index. Alderson, William Thomas, and Robert Hiram White, *A Guide to . . . Tennessee History.* Nashville: Tennessee Historical Commission, c. 1959. viii, 87 pp. Wickersham, James, *A Bibliography of Alaskan Literature, 1727–1924* . . . . Cordova, Alaska: Cordova Daily Times, 1927. xxvii, 635 pp.

k. Peterson, Clarence Stewart, *Bibliography of County Histories of the 3111 Counties in the United States.* 2d ed.; P. O. Box 342, Baltimore: Published by author, c. 1946. Supplements c. 1950, 1955, 1960.

l. Larned, Josephus Nelson, ed., *The Literature of American History: A Bibliographic Guide* . . . . Boston: Houghton Mifflin Co., 1902. ix, 596 pp. Continued by Philip P. Wells in *Titles of Books on English and American History;* New York: American Library Association, 1904; and A. L. A. *Booklist,* Feb. 1906.

m. George Washington University, Washington, D. C., *A Report on World Population Migrations as Related to the United States* . . . . Washington: George Washington University, c. 1956. Historical bibl., pp. 85–295, by Richard Catlin

Haskett. Also Dubester, Henry Joachim, *State Censuses: An Annotated Bibliography of Censuses of Population Taken after the Year 1790 by States and Territories of the United States.* Washington: Government Printing Office, 1948. v, 73 pp.

n. Evans, Charles, and Clifford Kenyon Shipton, *American Bibliography: A Chronological Dictionary of All Books, Pamphlets, and Periodical Publications Printed in the United States of America from the Genesis of Printing in 1639* . . . . [to 1800]. 14 vols.; New York: Peter Smith, 1941–59. Reprinted from edition begun in 1903. Author, subject, and publisher and printer indexes. Dr. Shipton, on behalf of the American Antiquarian Society and the American Historical Association, is editing the thirty thousand items listed in this bibliography — and in so doing correcting its many earlier errors — for microprinting by the Readex Microprint Corp., 115 University Place, New York 3. Price $8,000. See also Sabin, Joseph, Wilberforce Ames, and Robert William Glenroy Vail, *Bibliotheca Americana: A Dictionary of Books Relating to America from Its Discovery to* . . . [1860]. 29 vols.; New York: Bibliographical Society of America, 1868–1936. Austin, Robert B., *Early American Medical Imprints: A Guide to Works Printed in the United States, 1668–1920.* Washington: Government Printing Office, 1961. 250 pp. Appdx., index.

o. Billington, Ray Allen, *Westward Expansion: A History of the American Frontier.* 2d ed.; New York: Macmillan Co., 1960. Bibl. essay, pp. 762–854.

p. Clark, Thomas Dionysius, ed., *Travels in the Old South: A Bibliography.* 4 vols.; Norman: University of Oklahoma Press, c. 1948–59. Clark, *Travels in the New South* . . . . 2 vols.; *ibid.,* c. 1962. Also Hubach, Robert Rogers, *Early Midwestern Travel Narratives: An Annotated Bibliography, 1634–1850.* Detroit: Wayne State University Press, 1961. x, 149 pp.

q. Dumond, Dwight Lowell, *A Bibliography of Antislavery in America.* Ann Arbor: University of Michigan Press, c. 1961. 119 pp.

r. The *AHR* (see 2-A-2-m and 2-A-3-a, above), *The Mississippi Valley Historical Review,* with annual index, cumulated for first fifteen years and thereafter decennially, and *The Journal of Southern History,* with annual index (twenty-year cumulation in preparation) for reviews of books. Lists of articles in other journals in each issue but not included in indexes.

2. Periodical indexes.

a. Griffin, Appleton Prentiss Clark, *Bibliography of American Historical Societies,* published as Vol. II of the American Historical Association, *Annual Report, 1905.* Washington: Government Printing Office, 1907. 1,374 pp. Index and index of societies.

b. *Poole's Index to Periodical Literature.* (See 2-A-3-b, above.)

c. *Reader's Guide to Periodical Literature.* (See 2-A-3-c, above.)

d. *American Periodical Series.* Ann Arbor, Mich.: University Microfilms, 1947– . Annal. Cumulation anticipated.

e. Haskell, Daniel Carl, *The Nation, Volumes 1–105, New York, 1865–1917: Index of Titles and Contributors.* 2 vols.; New York: New York Public Library, 1951–53.

f. Mott, Frank Luther, *A History of American Magazines.* 4 vols. to date; Cambridge, Mass.: Harvard University Press, 1939– .

g. Doll, Eugene Edgar, *The Pennsylvania Magazine of History and Biography: Index, Volumes 1–75 (1877–1951).* Philadelphia: Historical Society of Pennsylvania, 1954. xv, 1,170 pp. Oldest existing historical magazine in the United States.

h. Leary, Lewis Gaston, *Articles on American Literature, 1900–1950.* Durham, N. C.: Duke University Press, 1954. 437 pp. Notes, index. Continued in annual supplements in *American Quarterly,* journal of the American Studies Association, covering also articles on other American fields and lists of dissertations in progress. See also Marshall, Thomas Frederic, *An Analytical Index to "American Literature,"* **Vols.** *I–XX (March 1929–January 1949)*. Durham, N. C.: Duke University Press, 1954. **viii,** 154 pp. Incl. book rev. index.

i. Winther, Oscar Osburn, *A Classified Bibliography of the Periodical Literature of the Trans-Mississippi West (1811–1957).* Indiana University Social Science Series, No. 19. Bloomington: Indiana University Press, 1961. xxvi, 626 pp. Index.

j. Arndt, Karl J. R., and May E. Olson, *German-American Newspapers and Periodicals, 1732–1955*. Heidelberg: Quell & Meyer; Worcester, Mass.: Clark University Press, 1961. 794 pp.

k. Rose, Fred Duane, *American Labor in Journals of History: A Bibliography*. Champaign: University of Illinois Institute of Labor and Industrial Relations, 1962. iv, 87 pp.

3. Newspaper indexes.

a. Cappon, Lester Jesse, and Stella F. Duff, *Virginia Gazette Index, 1736–1780*. 2 vols.; Williamsburg, Va.: Institute of Early American History and Culture, 1950. The newspaper itself can be obtained on microfilm at modest cost, as, indeed, can increasing numbers of historic newspapers. See Schwegmann, *Newspapers on Microfilm* (2-A-4-h, above).

b. *The New York Times Index*. (See 2-A-4-c, above.)

c. *New York Daily Tribune Index*. (See 2-A-4-d, above.)

d. Brayer, Herbert O., "Preliminary Guide to Indexed Newspapers in the United States, 1850–1900," *MVHR*, XXXIII (Sept. 1946), 237–58. (See 2-A-4-g, above.) Also *American Newspapers, 1821–1936 . . .* , ed. Winifred (Gregory) Gerould (2-A-4-f, above.)

e. Cohen, Hennig, *The South Carolina Gazette, 1732–1775*. Columbia: University of South Carolina Press, 1953. xv, 273 pp. A microfilm copy of all extant South Carolina newspapers, 1732–82, is obtainable from the Charleston Library Society in 12 reels for $150.00.

f. Footnotes in Carl Bridenbaugh, *Cities in the Wilderness* (reissue) and *Cities in Revolt* (notes issued separately in mimeographed form). New York: Alfred A. Knopf, 1955. Refer, by subject, to all colonial newspapers.

g. See *Public Opinion* (Washington and New York), 15 Apr. 1886, until absorbed after 30 June 1906 issue into *The Literary Digest,* 1 March 1890 through 19 Feb. 1938, for summaries of newspaper editorial opinion except in later years. Date of issue of quoted newspaper not customarily given. Included foreign press.

h. Crick, Bernard R., and Anne Dalthrop, *List of American Newspapers up to 1940 Held by Libraries in Great Britain and Ireland*. Edinburgh: British Association for American Studies, 1958. vi, 90 pp. Appdcs. Supplement No. 7 to BAAS, *Bulletin*.

4. Government documents.

a. Boyd, Anne Morris, *United States Government Publications . . . .* 3d ed., rev. by Rae Elizabeth Rips; New York: H. W. Wilson Co., 1949 [i. e., 1952]. xx, 627 pp. Bibls.

b. Schmeckebier, Laurence Frederick, and Roy B. Eastin, eds., *Government Publications and Their Use*. 3d ed., rev.; Washington: Brookings Institution, c. 1961. xi, 476 pp. Also Jones, James V., "Government Publications Useful for Research in American History," *The Historical Bulletin*, XXXII (Jan. 1954), 67–84. Annotated.

c. Poore, Benjamin Perley, *A Descriptive Catalogue of the Government Publications of the United States, September 5, 1774–March 4, 1881* (48th Cong., 2d Sess., Senate Misc. Doc. 67). Washington: Government Printing Office, 1885; Ann Arbor,

Mich.: J. W. Edwards, 1953. iv, 1,392 pp. Continued by U. S., Department of the Interior, Division of Documents, . . . *Comprehensive Index to the Publications of the United States Government, 1881–1893* (58th Cong., 2d Sess., House Doc. 754), by John Griffith Ames. 2 vols.; GPO, 1905. Republished, 2 vols. in 1; J. W. Edwards, 1953. Further continued by each Congress in *Catalog of the Public Documents* . . . . 25 vols.; Washington: Government Printing Office, 1896–1945. From 1940 it is necessary to use the *Monthly Catalog of United States Government Publications.* (Title varies.) Washington: Government Printing Office, 1895– .

d. Hirshberg, Herbert Simon, and Carl Herman Melinat, *Subject Guide to United States Government Publications.* Chicago: American Library Association, 1947. vii, 228 pp.

e. Powell, John Harvey, *The Books of a New Nation: United States Government Publications, 1774–1814.* Philadelphia: University of Pennsylvania Press, c. 1957. 170 pp. Also Childs, James B., "The Story of the United States Senate Documents, 1st Congress, 1st Session, New York, 1789," The Bibliographical Society of America, *Papers,* LVI (2d. quar., 1962), 175–94; and Tinling, Marion, Thomas Lloyd's Reports of the First Federal Congress," *The William and Mary Quarterly,* XVIII (Oct. 1961), 519–45.

f. National Archives and Record Service, Federal Register Division, *Public Papers of the Presidents of the United States,* 1957– . Washington: Government Printing Office, 1958– . Resumes, leaving a thirty-five-year hiatus, Richardson, James Daniel, ed., *A Compilation of the Messages and Papers of the Presidents, 1789–1897.* 10 vols.; Washington: Government Printing Office, 1896–99. Reprinted and extended to 31 March 1922, with notes, illus., maps, diagrs. in 20 vols. New York: Bureau of National Literature, Inc., n. d. Index — Vols. 19–20.

g. Hasse, Adelaide Rosalie, *Index to United States Documents Relating to Foreign Affairs, 1828–1861.* 3 vols.; Washington: Carnegie Institution of Washington, 1914–21. U. S., Department of State, *General Index to the Published Volumes of the Diplomatic Correspondence of the United States, 1861–1899.* Washington: Government Printing Office, 1902. 945 pp. Continued in *Papers Relating to the Foreign Relations of the United States: General Index, 1900–1918* (75th Cong., 3d Sess., House Doc. 714). *Ibid.,* 1946. iv, 507 pp. Thereafter must be pursued through tables of contents and indexes of the volumes of the *Foreign Relations of the United States; American Foreign Policy: Current Documents,* and other volumes of documents published by the Department of State. Supplement with Miller, Hunter, ed., *Treaties and Other International Acts of the United States of America.* Washington: Government Printing Office, 1931– . 8 vols., 1776–1863, to date, with efforts under way to continue in selective form. Vol. I (*Short Print*) *Plan of the Edition, Lists, and Tables.* x, 198 pp.

h. Bowker, Richard Rogers, *State Publications: A Provisional List of the Official Publications of the Several States of the United States from Their Organization.* New York: Publishers' Weekly, 1908. xii, 1,031 pp. National Association of State Libraries, *Collected Public Documents of the States: A Check List,* comp. William Sumner Jenkins. Boston, 1947. ix, 87 pp. National Association of State Libraries, Public Document Clearing House Committee, *Check List of Legislative Journals of the United States of America,* comp. Grace Elizabeth MacDonald. Rev. ed.; Providence, R. I.: Oxford Press, 1938. 1,274 pp. With supplement by William Sumner Jenkins. Boston, 1943. Also U. S., Library of Congress, *Monthly Checklist of State Publications,* 1910– . Washington: Government Printing Office, 1912– . With annual subject index. And *Check-List of Session Laws.* New York: H. W. Wilson Co., 1936. With frequent suppls. See also *The Territorial Papers of the United States,* original ed. Clarence Edwin Carter. Washington: Government Printing Office, 1934– .

i. Hasse, Adelaide Rosalie, *Index of Economic Material in Documents of the*

States of the United States. 16 vols.; Washington: Carnegie Institution, 1907–19. Covers thirteen Northern states.

j. Greene, Jack P., "Publication of Official Records of the Southern Colonies," *The William and Mary Quarterly,* XIV (Apr. 1957), 268–80. Jeffrey, William, Jr., "Early New England Court Records [1620–1800]: A Bibliography of Published Materials," in Boston Public Library, *Quarterly,* VI (July 1954), 160–84. Annotated.

k. There is no over-all or cumulative index of the debates of Congress, which must be pursued through the volumes and/or sessional reports of U. S., Constitutional Convention, 1787, *The Debates Reported by James Madison . . . ,* ed. Gaillard Hunt and James Brown Scott; U. S. Continental Congress, *Journals . . . , 1774–1789,* ed. Worthington Chauncey Ford, in 34 vols.; U. S., Congress, *The Debates and Proceedings . . . to May 27, 1824, Inclusive* [commonly known as the *Annals of Congress*], eds. Joseph Gales, Jr. and W. W. Seaton, in 42 vols.; U. S., Congress, *Register of Debates in Congress . . . ,* 1824 to 1837, eds. Gales and Seaton, in 19 vols. in 29; U. S., Congress, *Congressional Globe . . . ,* 1833 to 1873, eds. Francis Preston Blair, *et al.,* in 46 vols. in 111; and U. S., Congress, *Congressional Record,* 1873– .

5. Manuscripts.

a. Hamer, Philip May, ed., *A Guide to Archives and Manuscripts in the United States.* New Haven, Conn.: Yale University Press for the National Historical Publications Committee, 1961. xxiv, 775 pp. Index. Briefly describes collections of some 7,600 individuals listed in the *Dictionary of American Biography* (see 2-I-6-a, below) or similar works and having fifty or more items in one of approximately thirteen hundred depositories. Also U. S., Library of Congress, *The National Union Catalog of Manuscript Collections, 1959–1961 . . . .* Ann Arbor, Mich.: J. W. Edwards, Inc., 1962. viii, 1061 pp. Index. New accessions to be continued in periodic supplements. Microprinted from card file in Library of Congress covering twenty-four thousand collections in seventy-five cooperating libraries and archives, plus three thousand collections in LC, instituted under Lester Kruger Born. See also Hale, *Guide* (2-A-1-c, above) and Modern Language Association of America, American Literature Group, Committee on Manuscript Holdings, *American Literary Manuscripts: A Checklist of Holdings in Academic, Historical, and Public Libraries in the United States.* Austin: University of Texas, 1960. xxviii, 421 pp. Includes political and other materials.

b. *Guide to the Records in the National Archives.* Washington: Government Printing Office, 1948. xiv, 684 pp. Appdcs., index. With supplements (see *Publications of the National Archives and Record Service* — latest edition, March 1963, 10 pp. — available on request). See also *List of National Archives Microfilm Publications, 1961.* Washington: National Archives, 1961. vi, 231 pp., plus order forms. Index. Of particular use for biographies and local history are the original manuscript returns available on microfilm. Those available from 1800 through 1830 are listed, with prices, on pages 143–53 of the above booklet and for succeeding periods in *Federal Population Censuses, 1840–1880: A Price List of Microfilm Copies of the Original Population Schedules. Ibid.,* 1955. vi, 75 pp. In 1918–19, before the inception of the National Archives, the Bureau of the Census distributed the original schedules for agriculture, manufacturing, industry, social statistics, and defective, dependent, and delinquent classes, 1850–1880, to repositories in the respective states. The National Archives is now embarked on a program of obtaining photocopies of the returns that have survived this diaspora which will be available for purchase. See Franklin, William Neil, "Availability of Federal Population Census Schedules in the States," *The National Genealogical Society, Quarterly,* L (March, June 1962), 19–25, 101–109,. 127. See also *A Brief Guide to U. S. Naval Sources in the Washington D. C. Area.* Washington 15: Navy Department . . . Naval History Division. 1957. 7 pp. Also

Munden, Kenneth W., and Henry Putney Beers, *Guide to Federal Archives Relating to the Civil War*. Washington: National Archives, 1962. x, 721 pp. Index. Companion work on Confederate Archives in preparation — in meantime use Bethel, Elizabeth, *Preliminary Inventory of the War Department Collection of Confederate Records* (Record Group 109). *Ibid.*, 1957. x, 310 pp.

c. Garrison, Curtis Wiswell, "List of Manuscript Collections in the Library of Congress, July 1931," in American Historical Association, *Annual Report for the Year 1930*, I, 123–249; Powell, C. Percy, "List of Manuscript Collections Received in the Library of Congress, July 1931 to July 1938," *ibid.*, *1937*, I, 113–45; *Annual Report of the Librarian of Congress*, 1938–42; Library of Congress, *Quarterly Journal of Acquisitions*, 1943– . Under the direction of Public Law 85–147, 16 Aug. 1957, the LC is engaged in microfilming and indexing the collections of papers of twenty-three Presidents (Washington through Coolidge) in its Manuscript Division. See, for example, *Index to the Abraham Lincoln Papers*. Washington: Library of Congress, 1960. x, 124 pp. Prepared by Fred Shelley, Elizabeth M. Thomas, *et al.* The 97 reels of the Lincoln MSS may be purchased for about $765.00, or about $8.00 per individual reel.

d. Griffin, Grace Gardner, *A Guide to Manuscripts Relating to American History in British Repositories Reproduced for the Division of Manuscripts of the Library of Congress*. Washington: Library of Congress, 1946. xvi, 313 pp. Index.

e. Billington, Ray Allen, "Guides to American History Manuscript Collections in Libraries of the United States," *The Mississippi Valley Historical Review*, XXXVIII (Dec. 1951), 467–96.

f. Crick, Bernard R., and Miriam Alman, *A Guide to Manuscripts Relating to America in Great Britain and Ireland*. New York: Oxford University Press, for the British Association for American Studies, 1961. xxxvi, 667 pp. Notes, index. Between 1907 and 1937 the Carnegie Institution of Washington brought out a number of guides to materials for American history in archives in Great Britain, Canada, Spain, Mexico, Cuba, France, Germany, Austria, Switzerland, Italy, and Russia. See Handlin, *Harvard Guide* (2-I-1-a, above), pp. 87–88. Dr. Waldo G. Leland is at work on the completion of his volumes on materials in Paris. See also *The British Public Record Office: History, Description, Record Groups, Finding Aids, and Materials for American History, with Special Reference to Virginia*. Richmond: Virginia State Library, 1960. 178 pp. Also Born, Lester Kruger, *British Manuscripts Project: A Checklist of Microfilms Prepared in England and Wales for the American Council of Learned Societies, 1941–1945*. Washington: Library of Congress, 1955. xvii, 179 pp. The British Association for American Studies, under an advisory committee of Bernard R. Crick, *et al.*, has engaged Micro Methods Ltd. of London and Wakefield, Yorkshire, to microfilm a series of British records relating to American history.

g. Most of the state archives and the principal repositories of privately originated manuscript collections have prepared printed or mimeographed listings of their holdings. Information may be obtained by direct correspondence if you cannot find it otherwise. The issues of *The American Historical Review* and regional and state historical journals carry notices of the more important recent acquisitions. The Historical Records Survey of the Works Progress Administration inventoried many county and municipal archives. See Child, Sargent Bunage, and Dorothy P. Holmes, *Bibliography of Research Projects Reports: Check List of Historical Records Survey Publications*, Works Progress Administration, *Technical Series Research and Records Bibliography*, No. 7; Washington: Government Printing Office, 1943; 110 pp.; and Colby, Merle E., "Final Report on Disposition of Unpublished Materials of the W. P. A. Writers Program." In typescript, 1943. 12 pp. Virtually all of these W. P. A. publications are now out of print but are, along with the Child and Holmes and the Colby check lists, available in the Interior Section of the National Archives, with which arrangements may be made to obtain microfilm or photostatic reproductions.

See also Handlin, *et al., Harvard Guide* (2-I-1-a, above), pp. 79–88. See also Fox, Daniel M., "The Achievement of the Federal Writers' Project," *The American Quarterly,* XIII (Spring 1961), 3–19.

h. Jenkins, William Sumner, and Lillian A. Hamrick, *A Guide to Microfilm Collections of Early State Records.* Washington: Library of Congress, 1950. xxxviii, 308, 206, 44, 101, 56, 9, 38 pp. And *Supplement,* 1951. xxiii, 130, xxviii.

i. Greene, Evarts Boutell, and Richard Brandon Morris, *A Guide to the Principal Sources for Early American History (1600–1800) in the City of New York.* 2d ed.; New York: Columbia University Press, 1953. xxxvi, 400 pp. Continued in Carman, Harry James, and Arthur Webster Thompson, *et al., A Guide to the Principal Sources for American Civilization, 1800–1900, in the City of New York: Manuscripts. Ibid.,* 1960. xlviii, 453 pp.

j. *The Oral History Collection of Columbia University.* New York: Oral History Research Office, Columbia University, 1960. 111 pp.

k. Deutrich, Mabel E., *et al.,* "American Church Archives," *The American Archivist,* XXIV (Oct. 1961), 387–456.

l. Lewinson, Paul, and Morris Rieger, "Labor Union Records in the United States," *The American Archivist,* XXV (Jan. 1962), 39–45.

m. Kane, Lucile M., *A Guide to the Care and Administration of Manuscripts,* American Association for State and Local History, *Bulletin,* II, No. 11 (Sept. 1960) 333–88. Separately published.

6. Reference works and aids.

a. Johnson, Allen, and Dumas Malone, eds., *Dictionary of American Biography.* 21 vols., including index vol.; New York: Charles Scribner's Sons, 1928–37. Starr, Harris E., ed., *Dictionary of American Biography, Supplement One,* to 31 December 1935. *Ibid.,* 1944. 718 pp. Schuyler, Robert Livingston, and Edward Topping James, eds., . . . *Supplement Two,* to 31 December 1940. *Ibid.,* 1958. A condensed volume covering the whole is under way. *The Cyclopaedia of American Biography.* New enl. ed.; 6 vols.; New York: Press Associates, Compilers, Inc., 1915. Commonly known as "Appletons' Cyclopaedia of American Biography." Still useful for individuals not included in *DAB.*

b. *Who's Who in America.* Chicago: Marquis-Who's-Who, 1897– . Biennial. *Who Was Who in America.* Vol. I, 1897–1942; II, 1943–50; III, 1951–60. Chicago: A. N. Marquis, and Marquis Who's Who, Inc., 1943, 1950, 1962. See also regional (*Who's Who in New England, Who's Who in the South and Southwest, Who's Who in the West,* etc.), local, and occupational reference works compiled by this and other publishers. Keep in mind, however, that each sketch is usually autobiographical. Sibley, John Langdon, and Clifford Kenyon Shipton, *Biographical Sketches of Graduates of Harvard University* . . . . (Title varies.) Boston: Massachusetts Historical Society, 1879– . To date covers colonial period.

c. Cattell, Jaques, ed., *Directory of American Scholars: A Biographical Directory.* 3d ed.; New York: R. R. Bowker Co., 1957. x, 836 pp. New ed. in 4 vols. in preparation (Vol. I, *History,* in cooperation with Am. Hist. Assoc., Boyd C. Shafer, Executive Secretary; Vol. II, *English, Speech, and Drama;* III, *Foreign Languages: Modern and Classical;* IV, *Philosophy and Comparative Religion.*) *American Men of Science: A Biographical Dictionary.* 10th ed.; Tempe: Jaques Cattell Press, Inc., Arizona State University — *The Physical & Biological Sciences,* 4 vols., 1960–61; *The Social & Behavioral Sciences* scheduled for publication in 1962.

d. U. S., Congress, *Biographical Directory of the American Congress, 1774–1949* . . . . comp. James L. Harrison. (81st Cong., 2d Sess., House Doc., No. 607.) Washington: Government Printing Office, 1950. 2,057 pp. See also *Directory* for each Congress. Also U. S., Adjutant-General's Office, *Official Army Register;* also *Navy Register,*

Air Force Register, etc. U. S., Department of State, *The Biographic Register,* 1869– .
Washington: Department of State, 1869– . Annual, with gaps. First title, *Register
of the Department of State.* Issues for 1874, 1925–37, 1950, 1957 list ministers, am-
bassadors, etc. from the beginning arranged by countries. Also U. S., *Federal Register,*
14 March 1936– , issued daily by National Archives, publ. by GPO.

   e. Morris, Richard Brandon, ed., *Encyclopedia of American History.* Rev. ed.;
New York: Harper & Bros., 1961. xiv, 840 pp. Adams, James Truslow, and Roy V.
Coleman, eds., *Dictionary of American History.* 5 vols.; New York: Charles Scribners'
Sons, 1940. 6th suppl. vol. publ. 1961. Also *Id., Concise Dictionary of American
History,* Thomas C. Cochran and Wayne Andrews, eds. Scribners, 1962. Taken from
2,200 articles of original work.

   f. U. S., Bureau of the Census, *Historical Statistics of the United States, Colonial
Times to 1957: A Statistical Abstract Supplement.* Prepared with the cooperation of
the Social Science Research Council. Washington: Bureau of the Census, 1960. xi,
789 pp. Bibl. footnotes. *The Statistical Abstract of the United States* has been published annually since 1878. Bogue, Donald Joseph, *The Population of the United
States.* Glencoe, Ill.: Free Press, c. 1959. xix, 873 pp. Maps, diagrs., tables.

   g. *The World Almanac and Book of Facts,* 1869–77, 1887– . Also *Information
Please Almanac,* 1947– . Both annual. *The American Annual Cyclopaedia and
Register of Important Events,* 1861–1902. 42 vols.; New York: D. Appleton & Co.,
1865–1903. Known as "Appletons' Annual Cyclopaedia." 1st and 2d series have index
vols.; 3d series, cumulative indexes. *The* (New York) *Tribune Almanac,* 1856–1914;
successor to *The Whig Almanac . . . ,* 1838, 1843–55, and *The Politician's Register,*
1839–41. Particularly useful for election returns.

   h. Gohdes, Clarence Louis Frank, *Bibliographical Guide to the Study of the
Literature of the U. S. A.* Durham, N. C.: Duke University Press, c. 1959. ix, 102 pp.
Paperbound ed. Spiller, Robert Ernest, *et al., Literary History of the United States:
Bibliography.* New York: Macmillan Co., 1948. xxii, 817 pp. Index. Jones, Howard
Mumford, *Guide to American Literature and Its Backgrounds since 1890.* 2d ed., rev.;
Cambridge, Mass.: Harvard University Press, 1959. 192 pp. Paperbound. Hubbell, Jay
Broadus, *The South in American Literature, 1607–1900.* Durham, N. C.: Duke Uni-
versity Press, 1954. Bibl., pp. 883–974. Woodress, James, *Dissertations in American
Literature, 1891–1955, with Supplement, 1955–1961.* Durham, N. C.: Duke University
Press, 1962. xii, 138 pp. Index.

   i. Blanck, Jacob Nathaniel, *Bibliography of American Literature.* New Haven,
Conn.: Yale University Press, 1955– . Vol. III to "Bret Harte."

   j. Hart, James David, *The Oxford Companion to American Literature.* 3d ed.,
rev. and enl.; New York: Oxford University Press, 1956. viii, 890 pp. Chronological
index. Also *The Reader's Encyclopedia of American Literature,* ed. Max J. Herzberg,
et al. New York: Thomas Y. Crowell Co., c. 1962. ix, 1280 pp. Illus., ports.

   k. Mathews, Mitford McLeod, ed., *A Dictionary of Americanisms on Historical
Principles.* Chicago: University of Chicago Press, c. 1951. xvi, 1,946 pp.

   l. Wentworth, Harold, and Stuart Berg Flexner, *Dictionary of American Slang.*
New York: Thomas Y. Crowell Co., 1960. 669 pp. Wentworth, Harold, *American
Dialect Dictionary. Ibid.,* 1944. xv, 747 pp. Berrey, Lester V., and Melvin Van den
Bark, *The American Thesaurus of Slang: A Complete Reference Book of Colloquial
Speech.* 2d ed.; *Ibid.* c. 1953. xxxv, 1,272 pp.

   m. Shankle, George Earle, *American Nicknames: Their Origin and Significance.*
New York: H. W. Wilson Co., 1955. vii, 524 pp.

   n. [Plotkin, David George] David Kin, *A Dictionary of American Maxims.* New
York: Philosophical Library, c. 1955. 597 pp. Taylor, Archer, and Bartlett Jere Whiting, *A Dictionary of American Proverbs and Proverbial Phrases, 1820–1880.* Cambridge, Mass.: Belknap Press of Harvard University Press, 1958. xxii, 418 pp. Bibl.

Woods, Henry Fitzwilliam, *American Sayings: Famous Phrases, Slogans, Aphorisms.* New York: Duell, Sloan and Pearce, c. 1949. vi, 312 pp.

o. Silvestro, Clement M., and Sally Ann Davis, *Directory of Historical Societies and Agencies in the United States and Canada.* Madison, Wis.: American Association for the State and Local History, 1961– . Biennial publication planned. Preceded by earlier directories under same auspices. 111 pp. Also Silvestro, and Richard D. Williams, *A Look at Ourselves: A Report on the Survey of the State and Local Historical Agencies in the United States. Ibid.,* ix, 393–42.

p. Spear, Dorothea N., and Clarence Saunders Brigham, *Bibliography of American Directories through 1860.* Worcester, Mass.: American Antiquarian Society, 1961. 389 pp.

q. U. S., Navy Department, Chief of Naval Operations, Naval History Division, *Dictionary of American Fighting Ships.* Washington: Government Printing Office, 1959– .

r. New York Historical Society, *Dictionary of Artists in America, 1564–1860,* comps. George Cuthbert Groce and David H. Wallace. New Haven, Conn.: Yale University Press, 1957. xxvii, 759 pp. Mugridge, Donald Harold, *The Civil War in Pictures, 1861–1891; A Chronological List of Selected Pictorial Works.* Washington: Library of Congress, 1961. 30 pp.

s. Sperber, Hans, and Travis Trittschuh, *American Political Terms: An Historical Dictionary.* Detroit: Wayne State University Press, 1962. x, 516 pp.

7. Atlases.

a. Paullin, Charles Oscar, *Atlas of the Historical Geography of the United States.* Washington: Carnegie Institution . . . ; New York: American Geographical Society, 1932. xv, 162 pp., 166 plates. Index.

b. Adams, James Truslow, and R. V. Coleman, eds., *Atlas of American History.* New York: Charles Scribner's Sons, c. 1943. xi, 360 pp., 147 plates. Index.

c. Lord, Clifford Lee, and Elizabeth H. Lord, *Historical Atlas of the United States.* Rev. ed.; New York: Henry Holt & Co., c. 1953. xv, 238 pp. Maps, part colored.

d. Wesley, Edgar B., *Our United States: Its History in Maps.* Chicago: Denoyer-Geppert Co., c. 1956. 96 pp. Paperbound. *Hammond's American History Atlas.* Maplewood, N. J.: C. S. Hammond & Co., 1957. 30 pp. Paperbound.

e. Esposito, Vincent Joseph, chief ed., *The West Point Atlas of American Wars.* 2 vols.; New York: Frederick A. Praeger, c. 1959. Colored maps.

f. Cumming, William P., *The Southeast in Early Maps* . . . . 2d ed. with suppl.; Chapel Hill: University of North Carolina Press, 1962. 356 pp., 67 maps. Brown, Lloyd Arnold, *Early Maps of the Ohio Valley: A Selection of Maps, Plans, and Views Made by Indians and Colonials from 1673 to 1783.* Pittsburgh: University of Pittsburgh Press, c. 1959. xiv, 132 pp. 52 plates.

g. Sealock, Richard Burl, and Pauline Augusta Seely, *Bibliography of Place Names Literature — United States, Canada, Alaska, Newfoundland.* Chicago: American Library Association, 1948. 331 pp.

h. Gaustad, Edwin Scott, *Historical Atlas of Religion in America.* New York: Harper & Row, c. 1962. 179 pp. Maps, bibl.

J. LATIN AMERICA

1. Bibliographies.

a. Cline, Howard F., and Lon D. Hefner, "Latin America," pp. 355–414 in Am. Universities Field Staff, *Select Bibliography,* and pp. 47–58 in *Supplement, 1961* (2-A-2-f, above).

b. *Handbook of Latin American Studies . . . , 1935–* . Cambridge, Mass.: Harvard University Press, 1936–47; Gainesville: University of Florida Press, 1948– . Annual, succeeding Latin American section of *Writings on American History* (see 2-I-1-c, above).

c. *A Guide to the Official Publications of the Other American Republics.* 18 vols.; Washington: Library of Congress, Hispanic Foundation, 1945–48. There is one volume for each Latin American republic except Mexico and Nicaragua.

d. Jones, Cecil Knight, *A Bibliography of Latin American Bibliographies.* 2d ed.; Washington: Government Printing Office, 1942. 311 pp. Index.

e. Humphreys, Robert [i.e. Robin] Arthur, *Latin American History: A Guide to the Literature in English.* New York: Oxford University Press for Royal Institute of International Affairs, 1958. xiii, 197 pp.

f. Wilgus, Alva Curtis, *Histories and Historians of Hispanic America.* New York: H. W. Wilson Co., 1942. xii, 144 pp.

g. Harvard University, Bureau for Economic Research in Latin America, *The Economic Literature of Latin America,* comps. Clarence Henry Haring, *et al.* 2 vols.; Cambridge, Mass.: Harvard University Press, 1935.

h. Medina, José Toribio, *Biblioteca hispanoamericana, 1493–1810.* 7 vols.; facsimile ed.; Santiago, Chile: Fondo Histórico y Bibliográfico José Toribio Medina, 1958– . Originally publ., 1898–1907.

i. The New York Public Library, Reference Department, *Dictionary Catalogue of the History of the Americas Collection.* 28 vols.; Boston: G. K. Hall, 1961.

j. Bayitch, Stanley A., *Latin America: A Bibliographical Guide to Economy, History, Law, Politics, and Society.* Coral Gables, Fla.: University of Miami Press through New York: Oceana Publications, 1961. xv, 335 pp.

2. Current publications.

a. *The Hispanic American Historical Review* and *The American Historical Review* contain reviews of books and lists of articles since the latest issue of 2-J-1-b, above. See also Ruth Lapham Butler, *Guide to the Hispanic American Historical Review, 1918–45.* Durham, N. C.: Duke University Press, 1950. xviii, 251 pp. Continued in Gibson, Charles, and E. V. Niemeyer, *Id., 1946–55. Ibid.,* 1958. 178 pp. Index.

b. *Revista de historia de América.* Mexico, D. F.: Instituto Panamericano de Geografía e Historia, 1938– . Quarterly.

c. *Inter-American Review of Bibliography: Revista interamericana de bibliografía.* Washington: Pan American Union, 1949– . Quarterly.

d. *Américas.* Washington: Pan American Union, 1949– . Monthly. English, Spanish and Portuguese editions.

e. *Índice histórico español.* Barcelona: Editorial Teide, for the University of Barcelona, 1953– . Republished biennially in bound volumes as *Bibliografía histórica de España e Hispanoamérica.*

f. *Hispanic-American Report.* Stanford, Calif.: Stanford University Press, 1948– . Monthly. Title varies — 1948–49 *Hispanic World Report.*

3. Periodical indexes.

a. *Poole's Index to Periodical Literature.* (See 2-A-3-b, above.)

b. *Reader's Guide to Periodical Literature.* (See 2-A-3-c, above.)

c. *International Index to Periodicals.* (See 2-A-3-d, above.)

d. Zimmerman, Irene, *A Guide to Current Latin American Periodicals: Humanities and Social Services.* Gainesville, Fla.: Kallman Publ. Co., 1961. x, 357 pp.

4. Newspaper indexes.

a. *The Official Index to The Times* and *Palmer's Index to "The Times" Newspaper.* (See 2-A-4-b and 2-A-4-a, above.)

b. *The New York Times Index.* (See 2-A-4-c, above.)

c. *New York Daily Tribune Index.* (See 2-A-4-d, above.)

The above indexes are valuable because of the extensive Latin American coverage of these newspapers and also as guides to topics probably treated in leading Latin American dailies.

5. Manuscripts.

a. Hill, Roscoe R., *The National Archives of Latin America.* Cambridge: Harvard University Press, 1945. xx, 169 pp.

b. Hilton, Ronald, *Handbook of Hispanic Source Materials and Research Organizations in the United States.* 2d ed.; Stanford, Calif.: Stanford University Press, 1956. xiv, 448 pp. Index.

c. Harrison, John Parker, *Guide to Materials on Latin America in the National Archives.* 2 vols.; Washington: National Archives, 1961– .

e. Manuscript Division, Library of Congress. (See 2-I-5-b, above.)

d. Millares Carlo, Augustin, *Repertorio bibliográfico de los archivos mexicanos y de los europeos y norteamericanos de interés para la historia de México.* Mexico, D. F.: Biblioteca Nacional de México, Instituto Bibliografico Méxicano, 1959. xxiv, 366 pp.

f. Spain, Dirección General de Archivos y Bibliotecas, *Archivo General de Indias de Sevilla: Guía del Visitante,* by José María de la Peña y Cámara, Vol. XIII of Junta Técnica de Archivos, Bibliotecas y Museos, *Ediciones Commemorativas del Centenario del Cuerpo Facultativo, 1858–1958.* Madrid, 1958. 206 pp. Illus.

g. Gómez Canedo, Lino, *Los archivos de la historia de América: Perido colonial español.* 2 vols.; Mexico, D. F.: Instituto Panimericano de Geografía e Historia, Comisión de Historia, 1961.

6. Aids.

a. Martin, Percy Alvin, *Who's Who in Latin America.* 3d ed., rev. and enl.; 7 vols.; Chicago: A. N. Marquis Co.; London: Oxford University Press, 1946–51. By areas.

b. *Bibliography of Selected Statistical Sources of the American Nations.* Washington: Inter-American Statistical Institute, 1947. xvi, 689 pp.

3 NOTE TAKING

> *"Why," said the Gryphon, "you first form into a line along the sea-shore —"*
> *"Two lines!" cried the Mock Turtle. "Seals, turtles, salmon, and so on: then, when you've cleared all the jelly-fish out of the way —"*
> Lewis Carroll, *Alice's Adventures in Wonderland,*
> "The Lobster-Quadrille."

A proper note system, for both bibliographical and content notes, is an all but indispensable prerequisite to sound scholarship. Whenever your search brings you upon any item that seems to bear on your subject, first get a general conception of its theme and scope. With a book this normally means reading any prefatory material, examining the table of contents, then turning to the back to run through its bibliography, if it has one, and, finally, scanning the text, paying particular attention to the opening and concluding paragraphs of each chapter and to the topic sentences of other paragraphs. You will deal with an article or other short item in much the same way as you would a chapter, but somewhat more intensively.

1. Bibliographical cards. As soon as you are assured that an item will contribute materially to your investigation, make a bibliographical card for it. (Experienced historians sometimes also keep a special, or "Nix," file of works found valueless — the "jelly-fish" — as a reminder that they have consulted them.) You will later copy it into your final bibliography and must, therefore, follow the appropriate form in making it out. (See Ch. 5, sect. C, pars. 1–6, below.) Most historians use 3 × 5 cards for this purpose, lined or unlined according to whether they fill them out with pen or typewriter. Others, however, prefer 4 × 6 or even 5 × 8 cards in order to have more room for comments, and some use cards of different colors to indicate particular categories of material. Cards of any of these standard sizes, with lightweight metal filing boxes and alphabetical divider cards to match, can be procured easily and cheaply. Decide upon *one* size and use only that. Do not use a pencil unless the rules of the library where you are working require it; and in such a case it is generally best to spray with an artists' fixative or to recopy in more permanent form before it becomes illegibly smudged. *This applies also to content notes. See below.*

In addition to the information which you will include in your bibliography, note on each card the particular library in which you used it and the call number for convenience in later rechecking. After you have taken content notes (par. 2, below) on the item, use the remainder or back of the card to summarize the author's qualifications and point of view and your evaluation of the contribution that the item will probably make to your investigation. You will later use this information in preparing your annotated bibliography. Do *not,* however, try to make this serve the purpose of the content note or a substitute for it. You may get some assistance in evaluation from reviews of books in *The American Historical Review* and similar journals.

2. Content notes. You will set down in your content notes the substance of the working material that you are able to extract from your sources. First read through an entire chapter or article in order to gain a conception of its perspective and contours. If you find that you need only to note its purport in a general way, make a summary in outline form. If you need to record more detailed memoranda, do so in a series of notes, each of them dealing with a fairly specific point. Should you yield to the temptation to crowd several matters into a single note, you will later find that it contains information needed at different points in your narrative, with unimaginable inconvenience.

Different historians use a great variety of cards and slips of paper, varying to some extent in accordance with their fields of specialization. Choose whatever type is best suited to your own needs and then use it consistently. Do not try to take notes either in a bound notebook or on odd bits of paper. Cards of any of the three standard sizes indicated above for bibliographical notes are resistant to wear, but they are relatively expensive and because of their thickness take up more filing space. Pads of 5 × 8 inch paper are cheap and convenient. Try to use only one slip per note, using one side only, and tearing it off the pad for filing. If you must run over onto a second sheet, staple them together. Avoid paper clips, which are bulky, impede filing, and get lost. For long quotations it may be more convenient to use 8 × 10½ sheets of paper, one side only, which can then be folded to file with your regular sheets.

For convenience in filing: (1) set down in the upper left hand corner of the note the date, either specific or general as appropriate, of the occurrence referred to, followed by (2) the place, specific or general, where it took place, and (3) a caption summarizing the contents of the note that follows. On the next line cite the source, including pages. For example:

Fri., 12 Oct. 1492.   San Salvador (Watlings Is., Bahamas?).

Columbus First Sights Land.

John Knight, The History of Exploration in America (New York: Brown Co., 1927), p. 7.

(Summary)

Where you take only a few notes from any book or article, it will probably be more convenient to cite it in your note in precisely the same fashion in which you would refer to it in a footnote in your finished paper. (See 5-D, pars. 1–9, below.) If, however, you find it necessary to take numerous notes from the same source, you will probably find that it saves time to note down the source citation in an abbreviated form as you would do in the case of a second or subsequent footnote reference in your final paper. (See 5-D-12, below.) For example:

Knight, History of Exploration, p. 7.

In the margin indicate, possibly by an abbreviation or symbol, whether you have quoted your source verbatim or have summarized it. Do not use quotation marks, which might lead to confusion as to whether or not they appeared in the original. Verbatim notes should be taken sparingly — only when they may bear on a crucial point or contain a flavor worth preserving. A deletion must never change the meaning. Indicate it, *if within a sentence,* by three dots alternately spaced (thus . . .), and four if it follows a completed sentence (thus. . . .) — the first dot, of course being the period from the preceding sentence; and four also if your quotation ends in an unfinished sentence (thus . . . .) — the last dot being the period. Note space before first dot. Dots are not used at the beginning of a quotation that opens with a full sentence nor at the end of a quotation that closes with a full sentence. Check the note immediately to insure accuracy.

In cases in which you have to travel some distance to use the material, it is often cheaper as well as timesaving to arrange for photoduplication. You can generally have the repository make microfilmed or photostatic copies (the former being much less expensive but requiring a special machine for reading) or can secure permission to make photocopies with one of several devices now available which you may buy or borrow. Be sure to have one which can copy pages from books as well as separate sheets. Portable types, including developing fluid, are now obtainable.

3. Dates. The assignment of a date to an historical event may be quite complicated. Earlier dates were related to rulers and dynasties. In more recent times historians have attempted to fit all happenings to the Christian calendar. In 1582 Pope Gregory XIII proclaimed the Gregorian ("New Style," or "N. S.") Calendar, advancing ten days and providing for necessary future adjustments to bring the Julian ("Old Style" or "O. S.") Calendar into conformity with the solar year and fixing 1 January (earlier usually 25 March) as the beginning of the new year. Protestant England resisted the innovation until 1752, by which time it was necessary to advance eleven days. Dates for the intervening period are generally translated into New Style. Washington's Birthday of 11 February 1731 (or 1731/32), O. S. thus became 22 February 1732, N. S. "Perpetual calendars" are widely available to give you the day of the week if needed. It was not until about 1000 A.D. that dating the year from the presumed birth of Jesus came into general use. Non-Christian civilizations for convenience now generally use the Christian calendar, sometimes employing such euphemisms as "Before the Common Era" (B. C. E.) and "Common Era" (C. E.).

4 *CRITICISM*

Of some things I am not sure, but I am sure of one thing: that it is better and more manly to think that we ought to investigate what we do not know than idly to assume that we cannot, or ought not to, investigate. For this I would fight to the limit of my power in word and deed.
Plato, *Socratic Dialogues,* "Meno."

I have often said that the use of a university is to make young gentlemen as unlike their fathers as possible.
Woodrow Wilson, *Public Papers: The New Democracy,*
I, 199.

Your pursuit of evidence will have had much in common with a detective's search for clues. In the evaluation of the evidence which you uncover, you will follow rules of evidence comparable to those of a court of law. An obligation rests upon every historian as it does upon a member of a jury to render a verdict to the best of his ability solely in accordance with the evidence and with as full a sense of his responsibility. The development of the judicial process, although not yet free from the possibility of honest human error, has been the basis for security and freedom in human society. The historian's verdict upon which we base our evaluations of men and institutions of the past in order to see the present in perspective and attempt to prepare for the future can be, everything considered, at least as trustworthy as that of a court empowered to pass sentence on a man's property and life. It is not by chance that tyrants and demagogues seek both to subvert the courts and to pervert history. You will have to weigh conflicting evidence, discount special pleading, and bear in mind the fallibility of human observation and memory. And likewise your decision will be subject to review.

Although absolute truth may be an abstract ideal for human beings, you must never relax in the effort to attain it. If you make a sincere and wholehearted effort, avoiding easy excuses for your failures, you can achieve an objective attitude and approach a usable approximation of the truth.

The basic requirements are simple. Only four questions, each with its subquestions, must be answered:

1. Opportunity? Was the person who is your ultimate source of information in a position to observe the events he recorded? Was he intelligent and observant? Was he an insider? Did he have a background for understanding the event? If he got his information from someone else, all your criteria will have to be repeated for that person.

2. Objectivity? What sort of reputation did your informant have for honesty as well as intelligence? Was he known in his own circle as an addle-pated gossip who, like Eva the duck in one of James Thurber's "Further Fables for Our Time" (*The New Yorker,* 28 July 1956), "had two mouths but only one ear"? What were his prejudices and involvements of self-interest that must be discounted? As in the courtroom, an admission against self-interest, other things being equal, is most convincing. What sort of feeling do you get from the internal evidence of the record he has left as to his discernment and prob-ity? In time you will tend to acquire, as the result of experience stored up in your subconscious, a sort of sixth sense that will alert you to the telltale signs of a muddled or dishonest witness.

3. Transmission? Did your informant set down his observations imme-diately? Did he later rewrite them? Students of military history are familiar with the remark that on the day of battle Truth stands naked, but that as quickly as possible thereafter she begins to wrap herself in the garments of self-justification and myth. After the passage of even a single day a man's memory begins subtly to revise reality to magnify his own wisdom and the righteousness of his cause. Did your man record his information in a spirit of anger, apology, fear, despair, elation, or judicial calmness? To whom did he address himself? Was he writing to a confidant to whom he felt an obligation of candor or to someone whom he was trying to convince? If he spoke or wrote publicly, was his version challenged? Did he employ a ghost writer?

4. Meaning? You must always remain aware of the changing denotation and connotation of words — consulting where necessary dictionaries that indi-cate word meanings at various periods, and avoid pitfalls of irony and figures of speech. Beware of that worst of judicial sins — taking the evidence away from its context. Learn the special vocabularies and slang of different callings and levels of society. As you become saturated in some period of the past, you will be able to feel and think like men and women of that time and yet retain the critical perspective of your own.[10]

---

[10] We have not gone into the somewhat artificial distinction between "external" and "internal" evidence and other terms tending toward technical jargon. They are a heritage from German scholars who, influenced by Medieval Scholasticism, placed much emphasis on a categorization that both advanced and to some extent impeded the clarification of history as a scholarly discipline. Most notable of these men was Ernst Bernheim, whose *Lehrbuch der historischen Methode und Geschichtsphilosophie,* first published in 1889, reached a sixth edition at Leipzig in 1908. The French scholars Charles Victor Langlois and Charles Seignobos drew on Bernheim to some extent in their *Introduction aux études historiques* (Paris, 1898), which was translated into English by C. G. Berry and published as *Introduction to the Study of History* (New York: Henry Holt & Co., 1912). See also Louis Reichenthal Gottschalk, Clyde Kluckhohn, and Robert Angell, *The Use of Personal Documents in History, Anthropol-ogy, and Sociology . . . .* Social Science Research Council, *Bulletin 53* (New York: Social Science Research Council, 1945), xiv, 243 pp. On a specialized problem see Wilson R. Harrison, *Sus-pect Documents: Their Scientific Examination.* London: Sweet & Maxwell; New York: Frederick A. Praeger, 1958. 583 pp. Illus.

Yet here, Laertes? Aboard, aboard, for shame!
The wind sits in the shoulder of your sail, and you are stay'd
*   for.*
There; my blessing with thee!
And these few precepts in thy memory see thou character.
                          Hamlet, Act I, scene 3.

When you have exhaustively collected and carefully evaluated your evidence, you are ready to fit it together into a pattern of reconstructed truth. In this undertaking you will utilize to the full your powers of logical organization, integration, imaginative insight, and scholarly objectivity. You should be able to apply all, or most, of the following suggestions.

A. GENERAL

Leaving some of the more technical problems for discussion in later sections of this chapter, we need first to deal with four general procedures:

1. Outline. The primary secret of a well-constructed treatise is the fully integrated outline, arranged to trace the progress of your subject chronologically and by component topics and areas. You may find it best to open briefly with some dramatic and revealing event from the middle or end of your story and then turn back to the beginning of the developments that led to it. At the very inception of your research you will rough it out in preliminary form on the basis of your prior information, surmises, and unanswered questions. You will thereafter continually expand, revise, and rearrange it until you have completed the final version of a finished paper that represents the very best efforts of which you are capable. Always carry with you a note pad to jot down any sudden inspiration, either in the form of a concept or an illuminating phrase, that may unexpectedly arise out of the fermentation that will be taking place in your subconscious mind.

                           CONCLUSION

                           DISCUSSION

                         INTRODUCTION

The general structure of your outline and the research and writing that develop around that outline should be analogous to a fundamental artifact of modern building construction, the steel I-beam that, by replacing the solid wooden beams that once supported each floor of the structure, has made it feasible to erect buildings ten times the height of what was possible by earlier methods. Seen in cross-section, each such beam is broad at the base, as your introduction should be, so that it can rest firmly on the construction that preceded it; then it rises, as should discussion of the central theme of your study, as straightly narrow as possible in order to carry its proper burden without itself becoming cumbersome; and finally it, as will your conclusion, broadens out again to support further construction at the next level.

2. Note filing. In order to use your notes effectively you must be able to find them as you need them.

a. Bibliographical cards. File first in small metal boxes, obtainable at any stationery or variety store, that will hold about three hundred entries plus guide cards. As you continue your researches you can invest economically in a cardboard box file or in a double-drawered steel filing case that holds some three or four thousand cards. These cases are so designed that they will stack neatly on top of each other, as you acquire additional ones, to accommodate all the bibliographical cards that you are likely to accumulate in a lifetime of historical investigation. For any particular study you will file your cards alphabetically under the appropriate categories indicated in paragraph 5-E-17, below.

b. Content notes. An expanding cardboard file of appropriate size will suffice at first, but you may soon need to purchase a cardboard box file or a stackable double-drawered steel file, for which you can also buy a base. If you are filing your notes in folders you will need to get a 6 × 9 inch file to accommodate 5 × 8 inch notes. As your study develops you will file your content notes in tabbed sections (if on cards) or in folders (if on sheets of paper) in accordance with your outline, and refile them as you revise that outline. Finally each tabbed section or folder should represent a section or sub-section of your outline and correspond to a paragraph in your final paper.

3. Oral presentation. Before your research takes its final written form you may be called upon to present an oral report before a class, such as a research seminar, or to deliver a public lecture. The same essential organization should be followed in both oral and written presentation. But a somewhat different literary style is required for the ear than the eye, especially in the need for repetition — preferably by paraphrase — of key items of fact and interpretation that a reader could fix in his mind by rereading. (On the other hand it may be inadvisable during the course of composition to read your manuscript aloud, since the pauses and inflections of your voice may lend an emphasis and a clarity of meaning that will not be apparent in the cold print.) The most effective oral presentation is usually achieved by speaking informally, after thorough mental rehearsal, from a detailed outline. This outline should contain reference numbers, perhaps in red pencil, which will enable you to pick up without fumbling any of your reference notes that you plan to quote verbatim. If you try to read a formal paper aloud, except to a mature audience of fellow scholars, you are likely to lose contact with your audience. And any venture at talking directly from your notes is likely to degenerate into a rambling discourse. In a seminar you can assist your auditors by giving each member of the class (1) a brief typed outline, (2) a bibliography of your chief sources, and (3) a list of unfamiliar names and terms that you will use — and which you will have checked to insure correct pronunciation. Your classmates, in turn, can help you with their oral comments and, later, with written critiques. Avoid abruptly dramatic openings ("'The British are coming!' cried the hurrying horseman"); although occasionally suitable in print, where the eye anticipates what follows, they are likely to startle the ear.

4. Composition. You will construct the rough draft of your treatise paragraph by paragraph, guided by your outline. In writing each paragraph, first read over the notes contained in your folder or tabbed section. Then *close the folder and do not consult it again until you have finished your draft of the paragraph,* going back afterward to verify facts and to pick up overlooked points. If you attempt to work directly from your notes, one at a time, you are likely to produce a scrapbook rather than an original study in which you have distilled a new essence from your material.

Many writers find it best to write their first draft in longhand, continuing as long as their inspiration holds up and then pausing to copy each section on the typewriter, revising to some extent as they do and inserting footnote references (see 5-D, below, especially the unnumbered third paragraph). Some writers prefer not to insert footnotes until their final draft, instead placing corresponding numbers in the text and on each note to be cited in order to indicate the ultimate location. Type your drafts with double or triple spaces between the lines to leave room for corrections and interpolations. Always make a carbon copy and store it in a separate place as insurance against mishap. To avoid confusion you may wish to identify each draft or revision by some device such as jotting down on the corner of each page the date on which you prepared it. If you strike out a passage and then, after reconsideration, decide to retain it, write *stet* (from the Latin for "let it stand") beside it.

The number of drafts and revisions you will need to make will depend to some extent on the thoroughness with which you have mastered your subject. You may be both sobered and consoled to learn that many gifted and experienced writers have to rewrite again and again before they achieve the clarity and air of spontaneity at which they aim from the beginning.

B. QUOTATIONS

Quotations from the original sources or from authors of secondary works can help to point up your narrative if used with discriminating selectivity. (They have already been discussed to some extent in reference to note taking in Ch. 3, sect. 2, 4th par., above.) They are justified when they provide a special flavor from the original or bear upon some critical point that must be precisely demonstrated. Deletions must never change the original meaning. Indicate the deletion by three alternately spaced dots (thus . . .) if it is within a sentence, or by four if it immediately follows a completed sentence in the original (thus. . . .), the first one being the period belonging to that sentence, or (thus . . . .) if the quotation ends with an uncompleted sentence. Fit short prose quotations, preceded and followed by quotation marks, into your narrative in such a way as to preserve sentence capitalization if it is in the original. In such a case it would be — Captain John Knight replied, "Brave men will not surrender." If not — Captain John Knight replied that "brave men will not surrender." Quotation marks within the original are changed to single quotation marks (and, if absolutely unavoidable, a quotation within that quotation would be given double quotation marks), but otherwise the punctuation, capitalization, and spelling of the original should be followed wherever possible. This generalization would not hold if you were preparing a source book for undergraduates or the general reader. In such a case you would have reasonable leeway in modernization of punctuation and spelling to assist readability. Where you must interpolate an explanatory word or phrase of your own, place it in brackets. Parentheses are assumed to have been in the original. You can interpolate the notation "[*sic*]" in the text to show that the error it immediately follows is contained in the work you are quoting — thus protecting yourself from the assumption that it may be a factual or typographical error of your own.

1. Quotation marks. Note that periods and commas are always placed within the end quotation marks; colons and semicolons outside. Question marks, dashes, and exclamation points stand outside unless they are in the original.

2. Extensive quotations. A quotation of more than three lines should be set apart from your text by indenting it an additional four spaces and typing it single spaced — in contrast to the double spacing of your narrative text. (You will, of course, double space between paragraphs.) Use no quotation marks except as in the original. Indent four more spaces if you start with a paragraph beginning of the original, and do the same for subsequent paragraph beginnings. If the quotation begins within a sentence, do not capitalize the first word (unless, of course, it is a proper noun); and in this case the phrase of the text preceding it should not end with any punctuation mark, but should lead into it in the same manner as has been indicated for shorter quotations. Deletions within the quotation should also follow the same rules. Use common sense in paragraphing within it. Follow that within the original as closely as practical, but do not have broken lines straggling down a page.

In cases in which you are quoting *in extenso* — as, for example, in an appendix or in the compilation of a book of sources — you may run a line of dots, alternately spaced, from margin to margin to indicate the deletion of one or more paragraphs, either at the beginning, within, or at the end of your quotation. This is generally unnecessary in the case of fairly brief quotations in the midst of your text, where it would make for an unattractive appearance. You can, if you wish, indicate that the segments of your quotation are some distance apart in the original by interrupting the quotation with a line or so of text conveying this information. You will, however, need to use such a line of dots to indicate the deletion of one or more lines in the quotation of poetry.

In quoting, you must remember that the copyright holder has full ownership of the writing for twenty-eight years — fifty-six if he renews the copyright. It is advisable to secure his permission before including a quotation of any line of verse, particularly of copyrighted popular songs, or more than five lines of prose in any work you intend for publication. (If his address is unknown to you, it can be obtained from the publisher, who, indeed, will often obtain the consent for you if you explain the use you wish to make of it.) Consent is not needed for use of brief necessary quotations for purposes of rejoinder or in the writing of a book review, in which cases the courts assume "fair use" (Copyright Office, Library of Congress, circulars No. 20, 22, 91).

3. Foreign words. Quotations from foreign languages should, as a rule, be put into English that will as far as possible preserve the overtones as well as the literal meaning of the original. (See, for example, James Gauchez Anderson, *Le Mot Juste: A Dictionary of English and French Homonyms.* New York: E. P. Dutton & Co., c. 1938.) Short idiomatic phrases or terms of particular importance may be quoted in the original language if their meaning is explained. Do not give in to the temptation to flaunt your knowledge of Urdu or Chagatay; it will be sufficiently demonstrated by your references. When foreign words or phrases are set in a context of English, they should be underscored (italicized in a printed work) unless they are enclosed in quotation marks. This does not, of course, apply to names of people or places or to expressions which have become sufficiently anglicized as to be generally understood; in which case foreign accent markings are often not used. (When in doubt consult *Webster's Dictionary,* in which parallel bars in the margin or similar marks indicate the need for italicization.)

C. BIBLIOGRAPHICAL FORM

Reference has already been made in section 3–1, above, to the making out of bibliographical cards; and in section 5-E-17, below, the location of the bibliography in your completed paper is indicated.

There is no universally followed form for bibliographical entries. It would be all but impossible to prepare examples to cover every possible contingency. Two simple governing rules should be kept in mind: (1) the form used should be such as to enable anyone to look up the item cited with a minimum of difficulty and offer him a maximum of pertinent information consistent with brevity, and (2) any form and its necessary variations should be simple, logical, and consistent. Differences between the forms used for bibliographical items and footnote references should be the very minimum required by their differences in function. The following examples should enable anyone who keeps these principles in mind to adapt these forms to any unusual titles.[11]

1. Books.

The data following the date of publication below are not included in many systems, but are suggested here because of their usefulness to the reader. The example of annotation for an obviously fictitious title — as are most of

---

[11] Many helpful suggestions can be obtained from any of the following: Kate L. Turabian, *A Manual for Writers of Term Papers, Theses, and Dissertations* (rev. ed.; Chicago: University of Chicago Press, c. 1955), vii, 110 pp; William Riley Parker, "The MLA Style Sheet," *PMLA,* LXVI (Apr. 1951), 3–31 (also obtainable in separate form from 100 Washington Square East, New York 3); Griffith Thompson Pugh, *Guide to Research Writing* (Boston, etc.: Houghton Mifflin Co., c. 1955), 64 pp.; William Giles Campbell, *Form and Style in Thesis Writing (ibid.,* c. 1954), 114 pp.; Lucyle Hook and Mary Virginia Gaver, *The Research Paper* (2d ed.; New York: Prentice-Hall, Inc., 1952), 85 pp.; the volumes by Bauer, Hockett, and Kent referred to in footnote 8, above; and Oscar Handlin, *et al., Harvard Guide to American History* (Cambridge, Mass.: Belknap Press of Harvard University Press, 1954), pp. 38–44. In adhering to the principles stated above it has been necessary in the present booklet, after the most careful thought, to vary somewhat from the forms recommended by any one of them, as they do from each other. Clarence Edwin Carter, *Historical Editing* (National Archives, *Bulletin No. 7),* indispensable for its special purpose, represents decades of experience in the publication of official documents.

those that follow — will not herein be repeated for subsequent items. Words underscored in typing are italicized in print. Double underscoring indicates words to be set in small capital letters, and triple underscoring indicates full capitals. Sometimes, following the form used in the book you are listing, the pagination might run — xi, 693, x pp., or 11, 693, 10 pp.

Knight, John, <u>The History of Exploration in America</u>. New York: Brown Co., 1927. xi, 693 pp. Illus., maps, bibl., appdcs., index.

Awarded the Marco Polo prize. An exhaustive, unbiased treatment, based on research in principal European and North and South American archives. Propounds thesis that the spirit of adventure and the quest for economic advantage were equally essential in the opening up of the New World.

---

a. Variations in authorship. To aid your reader to find the book as conveniently as possible, give the author's full name, if ascertainable, regardless of how it may appear on the title page. Catalogue cards, printed by the Library of Congress and used by most other libraries, usually contain this information. To avoid confusion concerning authors of identical names you may indicate their dates of birth — Knight, John (b. 1883) or (1883-1948) or include an appropriate explanation in your bibliography and first footnote references.

(1) *Do not use titles or suffixes* (Prof., Gen., Dr., Msgr., Ph.D., S.J., etc.) unless to prevent confusion through lack of needed information — Knight, Mrs. John; or MacAnridire, Sister John the Baptist — but Knight, Jane (Squire); MacAnridire, Mary Magdalen; Knight, John, Jr.; Knight, John, III (more logical), or Knight, John III (more usual practice). A nobleman may properly be listed under his title — Herrenburg, Jakob Karl Junker, 8th Baron von. Chinese and certain other Oriental names (especially Japanese, Korean, and Vietnamese) in which that of the family comes first — Sun Yat Sen — are not reversed. In a Western context, however, many avoid confusion by consolidating the personal names — Lin Yutang — or by adopting the order to which we are accustomed — Chen Ning Yang. Many make this clearer by hyphenating the personal names — Tsung-Dao Lee — and some do not capitalize the second — Lien-sheng Yang. Still others prefer initials — T. V. Soong. *For bibliographical purposes* all such names should be given in a single standard form — Sun, Yat-sen — Lin, Yu-t'ang — Yang, Chen-ning — Lee, Tsung-dao — Soong, Tse-ven, etc. (In footnotes it would be Sun Yat-sen,

Lin Yutang, Tsung-dao Lee, T. V. [Tse-ven] Soong, Chen-ning Yang, etc.) Hispanic names — Juan Diego Francisco Caballero [father's name] Hidalgo [mother's name] — in a bibliography — Caballero Hidalgo, Juan Diego Francisco. Sometimes the two family names are hyphenated — Caballero-Hidalgo — or written — Caballero y Hidalgo. In social usage some dispense with the mother's name, and a few, where it may be especially prestigious, emphasize it to the extent of treating the paternal as though a middle name; but the standard form indicated above is to be followed, nevertheless, in a bibliography. A few British choose to dispense with the hyphen, generally employed in comparable names, in their surnames (Basil Hart Liddell Hart, or see Chapter 2, paragraph E-1-a, above).

(2) *If no author's name is given* on the title page but it can be ascertained from other sources, enclose it in brackets. A pseudonym should be preceded by the real name in brackets — [Knight, John] Gaylord Chevalier — and alphabetized under it. If the author is unknown, list alphabetically under the first word of the title after the article (*a, an, the, le, der,* etc.), if any.

(3) *Multiple authors.* Two authors — Knight, John, and James Charles Squire, The History .... Since the item will be filed and listed under the name of the first author given, there is no need to reverse the normal order for other names. Three authors — Knight, John, James Charles Squire, and George D. Page. The assumption here is that Knight has no ascertainable middle name and that it has been possible to discover only the middle initial for Page. Four or more authors — Knight, John, et al., The History .... Even if the authors should be related, each will be given his full name — Knight, John, and Jane (Squire) Knight.

(4) *Organization as author.*
Middle States Historical Association, Annual Report for the Year 1955. Crossways, Del.: Nonesuch Publishers, 1956. 213 pp. Index.

(5) *Editorship.* If a book, written by one man, is subsequently edited by another it would be — Morgan, Lewis Henry, The Indian Journals, 1859-62, ed. Leslie A. White. Ann Arbor: University of Michigan Press, c. 1959. 229 pp. Illus., maps. (This is not a fictional title.) If, however, it is the work of several contemporary authors or a collection of selected sources — it appears under the editor's name in the same manner as if he were the author — Knight, John, ed., The History .... — Knight, John, and James Charles Squire, eds., The History ....

(6) *Translators' names follow the title.*
Ritter, Johann, The History of Exploration in America, trans. [or — trans., with notes,] James Charles Squire. New York: Brown Co., 1927. xxi, 963 pp. Maps, bibl., index.

b. **Variations in title.**

(1) *In Romance languages, Swedish,* and *Russian* only proper nouns and the first word of the title and subtitle are capitalized. French authors sometimes exercise an option to capitalize other significant words.

Chevalier, Jean, Histoire de l'exploration en Amérique.

(2) *In German, Dutch, Danish,* and *Polish* the first word of the title and subtitle and all nouns and words used as nouns (plus, in Dutch, adjectives derived from proper nouns and, in German, adjectives derived from the names of persons) are capitalized. In *Latin* all proper nouns and adjectives derived therefrom are capitalized.

Ritter, Johann, Geschichte der Erforschung in Amerika.

An alternative system, especially desirable for words adapted from other alphabets, is to use the English system of capitalization for all foreign book titles.

(3) *Titles in languages generally unfamiliar* should be followed by an English translation in brackets.

Bogatyr, Ivan, Istoriia issledovania v Amerike [The history of exploration in America].

(4) *Subtitles* are treated in the same fashion as titles.

Knight, John, The History of Exploration in America: An Adventure during Four Centuries.

You are not bound in any case by the punctuation you find on the title page, but should follow a standard system.

(5) *Volume in a series.*

Knight, John, The History of Exploration in America, Vol. IV of The Saga of Mankind, ed. James Charles Squire. New York: Brown Co., 1927. xi, 693 pp. Illus., maps, bibl., appdcs., index. Part of a series that is an integrated work.

Knight, John, The History of Exploration in America. Studies in History Edited by the Faculty of the Graduate School of the Central University of America, Vol. XXXI, No. 3. Centralia, Mo.: Central University of America Press, 1927. xi, 693 pp. Illus., maps, bibl., appdcs., index. For a volume in an indefinite series.

Sometimes publishers carry a half-title page, preceding the title page, or may carry it at the top of the title page, bearing a rather general title such as "Brown Studies in History." In most cases it may be disregarded.

c. Variations in publishing data.

(1) *Subsequent editions.*

Knight, John, The History of Exploration in America. Rev. ed.; New York: Brown Co., 1934. xxii, 693 pp. Maps, bibl., index. or

Knight, John, The History of Exploration in America. 2d ed. rev. and enl.; New York: Brown Co., 1934. xxii, 739 pp. Bibl., index.

(2) *Multiple volumes.*

Knight, John, The History of Exploration in America. 2nd ed; 6 vols.; New York: Brown Co., 1925-28. Illus., maps, bibl. No indication of number of pages is, as a rule, needed for multiple volumes, since substantial size is suggested.

(3) *Place of publication.*

If the publisher maintains major offices in two cities, they may be indicated in this fashion — New York & San Francisco: Brown Co., 1927. If three or more are listed, select the first or the one most featured — New York, etc.: Brown Co., 1927. If place of publication is not indicated but is known from other sources — [New York:] Brown Co., 1927. If it is unknown — n. p., — for "no place" — Ocre Co., 1927, or [1927?] if date is inferred. Omit state (and nation) of major cities and for state publications and state university presses if it is repetitive.

There appears to be a growing disposition to regard the indication of place of publication (which once suggested the likelihood of national or regional bias) for university presses and the better known modern commercial publishers in the United States as superfluous, but its deletion has not yet become general.

(4) *Publisher's designation.* The practice of giving the name of the publisher (in earlier times often simply a job printer) although still not universal, is now widespread and in many cases is beyond argument, especially in more recent publications. The imprint of a respected publishing house or university press tends, with occasional lapses, to carry an assumption of responsibility, while that of certain others should alert the experienced reader to be on guard against special pleading.

If "The Brown Company" were differently styled it might be one of the following — Brown Bros. Co.; Z. Brown & Sons, Ltd. (Ltd. usually indicates a corporation in the British Commonwealth); or Brown & Green.

If the publisher is not given but is known from other sources, place in brackets. If unknown — New York: privately printed, 1927.

(5) *Date of publication.*

If no date of publication is given, use copyright date on the back of the title page — New York: Brown Co., c. 1927. If neither is given but one is known from other sources, place in brackets. If both are unknown — New York: Brown Co., n.d. — for "no date."

2. Public documents.

In citing public documents and corporate publications the writer must constantly remind himself of his responsibility to those readers who will wish to go to his sources. He should, therefore, find and follow the *main entry card,* which is printed and distributed to other libraries by the Library of Congress — ignoring any cross-reference heading which may be typed at the top of the card. The main entries may also be found in the book catalogues (see 2-A-1) published by the LC. This would be relatively simple if the following logical rules had been consistently observed: The primary citation should be given (1) where possible, by individual author, editor, or compiler — both for ease in finding and in justice to the author; or, (2) where not possible, by citation of the organizational author. In this case the nation, state, city, or business corporation, should be given first and followed by the major divisions and intermediate subdivisions to the ultimate responsible unit (without losing the searcher in an intramural labyrinth). Unfortunately, as some of the following examples (and those to be found scattered through the bibliographies in Chapter 2) will demonstrate, the vagaries of cataloguing (and cataloguers) often unnecessarily complicate the search. After looking under all headings that ingenuity can suggest, seek the aid of a reference librarian fortified by experience and gifted with second sight. (See also comment at end of 2-A-1.)

    a. Legislative debates.

    U. S., Continental Congress, Journals . . . , 1774-1789, ed. Worthington Chauncey Ford, et al. 34 vols.; Washington: Government Printing Office, 1904-37. Facsims.

The practice now followed by the GPO of placing "U. S." before its name need not be followed. "G. P. O.," or "GPO," may, indeed, be used, if consistently.

    U. S., Congress, Congressional Record . . . , 1873- . Washington: Government Printing Office, 1873- .

It is unnecessary to give the full title of so standard a publication.

    Parliamentary History of England from the Norman Conquest in 1066 to the Year 1803, eds. William Cobbett and J. Wright. 36 vols.; London: T. C. Hansard, 1806-20.

    Great Britain, Parliament, Parliamentary Debates . . . . 5th ser. (28th Parl., 4th sess., 9 Edward VII, 16 Feb. 1909-). London: H. M. Stationery Office, 1909- . Known, especially to 1891, as "Hansard's Debates," or simply "Hansard's," from the printer given in the preceding item.

The problem of changing the reference from "His Majesty's Stationery Office" to "Her Majesty's . . ." when a woman succeeds to the throne makes the standard use of the abbreviation advisable. "H. M. S. O." or "HMSO" may be used.

    [Le Moniteur Universel:] Réimpression de l'ancien Moniteur . . . (mai 1789-novembre 1799) . . . . 32 vols.; Paris: Henri Plom, printer-editor, 1858-63.

    Archives parlementaires, de 1787 a 1860: Recueil complet des débats legislatifs & politiques des chambres françaises. Ser. II, 1800-1860 (completed to 17 July 1839), eds. Jéromé Madival, Èmile Laurent, et al. 127 vols.; Paris: Paul Dupont, 1879-1913.

    France, Journal Officiel: Débats Parlementaires — Chambre de Députés Debáts, Session Ordinaire, 13 Jan.-15 July 1914. 3 vols., plus 2 vols. of documents.

    Germany, Stenographische Berichte über die Verhandlungen des Reichstages . . . , 1871-1942. Berlin, 1871-1942.

    Germany (Federal Republic,1949-), Bundestag, Verhandlungen: Stenographische Berichte, Sept. 7, 1949- . Berlin, 1949- .

    Belgium, Moniteur Belge — Belgisch Staatsblad: Journal Officiel — Staatsblad. (Débats, lois, arrêtés royaux et du gouvernement, documents, etc.) Brussels, etc., 1831.

Virginia, General Assembly, 1790-1800, House of Delegates, <u>Alien</u> <u>and</u> <u>Sedition</u> <u>Laws</u>: <u>Debates</u> <u>in</u> <u>the</u> <u>House</u> <u>of</u> <u>Delegates</u> <u>of</u> <u>Virginia</u> <u>in</u> <u>December</u>, <u>1799</u>, <u>on</u> <u>Resolutions</u> <u>before</u> <u>the</u> <u>House</u> <u>on</u> <u>Acts</u> <u>of</u> <u>Congress</u> <u>Called</u> <u>the</u> <u>Alien</u> <u>and</u> <u>Sedition</u> <u>Laws.</u> (Prepared for the United States Senate, 62d Congress, 2d sess., Senate Doc. 873.) Washington: Government Printing Office, 1911. 187 pp.

b. Legislative documents, hearings, reports, law memoranda.

U. S., 49th Congress, 1st Session, 1885-1886 . . . , <u>Memorial</u> <u>Addresses</u> <u>on</u> <u>the</u> <u>Life</u> <u>and</u> <u>Character</u> <u>of</u> <u>Thomas</u> <u>A.</u> <u>Hendricks</u> (<u>Vice-</u> <u>President</u> <u>of</u> <u>the</u> <u>United</u> <u>States</u>), <u>Delivered</u> <u>in</u> <u>the</u> <u>Senate</u> <u>and</u> <u>House</u> <u>of</u> <u>Representatives.</u> (49th Cong., 1st sess., Senate, Misc. Doc. 120.) Washington: Government Printing Office, 1886. 168 pp.

U. S., Congress, Joint Committee on Foreign Economic Cooperation, <u>Report</u> <u>on</u> <u>Progress</u> <u>of</u> <u>the</u> <u>Economic</u> <u>Cooperation</u> <u>Administration</u> . . . . (81st. Cong., 1st sess., 1949, Senate Report 13, Serial no. 11291.) Washington: Government Printing Office, 1949. ix, 152 pp.

Note that wherever possible the name of the committee (the work of which may continue over several sessions) takes precedence; but session and document numbers should also be given, since libraries generally file them in this manner.

U. S., Congress, House, Committee on Ways and Means, <u>Foreign</u> <u>Trade</u> <u>Policy</u>: <u>Hearings</u> <u>before</u> <u>the</u> <u>Subcommittee</u> <u>on</u> <u>Foreign</u> <u>Trade</u> <u>Policy</u>, . . . <u>Dec.</u> <u>2-13</u>, <u>1937</u>, pursuant to House Resolution 104. (85th Cong., 1st sess.) Washington: Government Printing Office, 1938. vi, 865 pp. Diagrs., tables.

U. S., Congress, Senate, Committee on Education and Labor, <u>Violations</u> <u>of</u> <u>Free</u> <u>Speech</u> <u>and</u> <u>Rights</u> <u>of</u> <u>Labor</u>: <u>Industrial</u> <u>Munitions</u>. (76th Cong. 1st sess., Senate Report 6, part 3, March 20 [legislative day March 16], 1939, pursuant to Senate Resolution 266, 74th Cong.) Washington: Government Printing Office, 1939. iv, 240 pp. Illus., appdcs., index.

Note that it has been found useful to arrange this citation somewhat differently than some preceding and following it. This is permissible where logical, and if the correct primary heading is preserved. Brackets are necessary, to avoid confusion, within parentheses.

U. S., Congress, House, Committee on Agriculture, <u>Hearings</u> . . . <u>General</u> <u>Farm</u> <u>Problem</u>, part 2, April 7, 11, 12, 25, 26, 1949 (Serial P). (81st Cong., 1st sess.) Washington: Government Printing Office, 1949. iii, 187-357 pp.

U. S., Congress, Senate, Committee on Printing . . . , <u>The</u> <u>Printing</u> <u>Industry</u> <u>and</u> <u>the</u> <u>Proposed</u> <u>Copyright</u> <u>Convention</u>: <u>Memoran-</u> <u>dum</u> <u>Regarding</u> <u>Probable</u> <u>Effects</u> <u>on</u> <u>the</u> <u>Printing</u> <u>Industry</u> <u>of</u> <u>Adoption</u> <u>of</u> <u>the</u> <u>Copyright</u> <u>Convention</u> . . . , presented by Mr. Hayden. Ordered printed July 20 (legislative day July 18), 1939. (76th Cong., 1st sess., Senate Doc. 99.) Washington: Government Printing Office, 1939. iii, 19 pp. Tables.

U. S., Congress, House, Committee on Public Works, National
Highway Program: Hearings . . . On H. R. 4260, to Create a Federal
Highway Corporation for Financing the Construction of the National
System of Interstate Highways; to Amend and Supplement the Federal-
Aid Road Act Approved July 11, 1916 (39 Stat. 355), as Amended
and Supplemented, and for Other Purposes . . . . (84th Cong., 1st
sess.) 2 pts.; Washington: Government Printing Office, 1955. vii,
1,339 pp. Illus., maps.

Great Britain, Royal Commission on the Civil Service (1953-
55), Report. (Parliament, 1955-56 sess., Vol. XI, 925 ff., Papers
by Command, cmd. 9613.) London: H. M. Stationery Office [1955].
viii, 238 pp. Tables.

The Command Papers, prepared in theory on the monarch's authority, are
numbered in four separate series, identified by "c." to 1900, "cd." 1900–1919,
"cmd." 1919–56, and "cmnd." 1956– .

Great Britain, West India Royal Commission (1938-39), Statement
of action Taken on the Recommendations . . . . ([Parliament, Papers
by Command] cmd. 6656.)

Great Britain, Committee of Inquiry on the Rehabilitation,
Training, and Resettlement of Disabled Persons, Report. (Parliament,
Papers by Command, cmd. 9883.) London: H. M. Stationery Office
[1956].) v, 126 pp.

Great Britain, Ministry of Local Government and Planning, Town
and Country Planning, 1943-1951: Progress Report . . . . ([Parlia-
ment, Papers by Command] cmd. 8204.)

c. Constitutions and statutes.

U. S., Articles of Confederation, The Exact Text of the Articles
of Confederation, with the Franklin and Dickinson Drafts, from the
Original Manuscripts. American History Leaflets, No. 20, eds.
Albert Bushnell Hart and Edward Channing. New York: A. Lovell &
Co., 1895. 27 pp.

U. S., Constitution, The Constitution of the United States of
America, as Amended to December 1, 1924, Annotated; with Citations
to the Cases of the Supreme Court of the United States Construing
Its Several Provisions Collated under Each Provision. (68th Cong.,
1st sess., Senate Doc. 154.) Washington: Government Printing
Office, 1924. iii, 876 pp.

U. S., Laws, Statutes, etc., Tariff Acts Passed by the Congress
of the United States from 1789 to 1897, including All Acts, Reso-
lutions and Proclamations Modifying or Changing Those Acts, compiled and indexed under the direction of the Joint Committee on
Printing by Robert G. Proctor. (55th Cong., 2d sess., House Doc.
562.) Washington: Government Printing Office, 1898. 689 pp.

U. S., Laws, Statutes, etc., An Act to Amend the Interstate
Commerce Act, as Amended, So as to Strengthen and Improve the National Transportation System and for Other Purposes. Public Law

85-625. (85th Cong., S. 3778, Aug. 12, 1958.) Washington: [Government Printing Office] 1958. 7 pp.

France, Laws, Statutes, etc., _Loi du 11 juillet 1938 sur l'organisation generale de la nation pour les temps de guerre_. Paris: Centres d'Information Interprofessionne, c. 1942. 30 pp.

District of Columbia, Laws, Statutes, etc., _District of Columbia Code_. 1940 ed. . . . ; 2 vols.; Washington: Government Printing Office, 1941.

d. Executive documents.

U. S., War Department, _The War of the Rebellion: A Compilation of the Official Records of the Union and Confederate Armies_ . . . (U. S., Congress, 52d-56th Cong., House Misc. Doc.) 70 vols. in 128; Washington: Government Printing Office, 1880-1901.

U. S., Maritime Administration, _A Review of Maritime Subsidy Policy in the Light of Present National Requirements for a Merchant Marine and a Shipbuilding Industry_. [Committee on] Merchant Marine and Fisheries, House of Representatives (83d Cong., 2d sess.). Compare with references under _b._, above.

U. S., Department of State, "_I'm Alone_" _Case_ . . . . Publications of the Department of State, Nos. 210, 209, 208, 464, 442, 748, 711. (Arbitration Series, No. 2). Washington: Government Printing Office, 1931-35. Illus., tables.

U. S., Census Office, 7th Census, 1850, _The Seventh Census of the United States, 1850 Embracing a Statistical View of Each of the States and Territories, Arranged by Counties, Towns, etc._ . . . _and an Appendix Embracing Notes upon the Tables of Each of the States, etc._ . . . , by J. D. B. DeBow, Superintendent of the United States Census. Washington: R. Armstrong, Public Printer, 1853. cxxvi, 1022 pp.
Became Bureau of the Census in 1902.

U. S., Bureau of Mines, _Analyses of Pennsylvania Bituminous Coals_. (Technical Paper 590.) Washington: Government Printing Office, 1939. iv, 503 pp. Illus., maps, table, diagr.

In the case of a bureau as author, the department of government in which it is located is, illogically, omitted. It is generally given in the case of smaller subdivisions.

U. S., Library of Congress, Legislative Reference Service, . . . _Income Tax in Great Britain, Including a Description of Other Inland Revenue Taxes_. Prepared for the Joint Committee on Internal Revenue taxation by André Bernard under direction of H. H. B. Meyer, Director of Legislative Reference Services, Library of Congress. (70th Cong., 1st sess., House Doc. 332.) Washington: Government Printing Office, 1928. xviii, 226 pp. Tables, diagr.

U. S., Attorney General's National Committee to Study the Antitrust Laws, _Report_. [Washington: Government Printing Office] 1955. xiii, 393 pp.

Heer, Clarence, Federal Aid and the Tax Problem. U. S. Advisory Committee on Education, Staff Study, No. 4. Washington: Government Printing Office, 1939. ix, 101 pp. Tables, diagrs.

Pogue, Forrest C., The Supreme Command (United States Army in World War II: The European Theater of Operations). Washington: Office of the Chief of Military History, Dept. of the Army, 1954. xxi, 607 pp. Illus., maps, bibl.

The degree to which a series title may be deemed parenthetical must sometimes be decided on a pragmatic basis.

Great Britain, Foreign Office, Documents on British Foreign Policy, 1919-1939, eds. Ernest Llewellyn Woodward . . . and Rohan d'Olier Butler . . . . London: H. M. Stationery Office, 1946- .

Great Britain, Foreign Office, Historical Section, Abyssinia. Handbook No. 129. (Peace Handbooks, Vol. XX, No. 8.) London: H. M. Stationery Office, 1920. 109 pp.

Great Britain, Exchequer, The Great Roll of the Pipe for the Fourteenth Year of the Reign of King Henry the third, Michaelmas 1230 (Pipe Roll 74), Now Printed from the Original in the Custody of the Right Hon., the Master of the Rolls, ed. Chalfant Robinson . . . . Princeton, N. J.: Princeton University Press, 1927. xxxii, 472 pp.

Great Britain, Curia Regis, Curia Regis Rolls . . . Preserved in the Public Record Office . . . . London: H. M. Stationery Office, 1922- .

France, Ministère des Affaires étrangères . . . , Documents diplomatiques: 1861. Paris: Imprimerie Imperiale, 1867. 132 pp.

France, Archives des Affaires étrangères, Inventaire sommaire des archives du Département des affaires étrangères: Mémoires et documents . . . . 3 vols.; Paris: Imprimerie Nationale, 1883-96.

Illinois, Department of Public Works and Buildings, New Salem (New Salem State Park, near Petersburg, Illinois): A Memorial to Abraham Lincoln (Half-title: Catalogue of New Salem Collection of Pioneer Relics.) 6th ed.; [Springfield] 1947. vii, 184 pp. Plates.

New York (State), Commission on Old Age Security, Old Age Security: Report of the State Commission, Transmitted to the Legislature, February 17, 1930. (Legislative Document [1930], No. 67.) Albany: J. B. Lyon Co., 1930. 692 pp. Tables, diagrs., forms.

New York (City), Burgomasters and Schepens, The Records of New Amsterdam from 1653 to 1674 Anno Domini, ed. Berthold Fernow. 7 vols.; New York: Knickerbocker Press, under authority of the city, 1897.

League of Nations, Mixed Committee on the Problem of Nutrition, Final Report . . . on the Relation of Nutrition to Health, Agriculture, and Economic Policy (A.13.1937.II.A). Geneva, 1937. 327 pp.

United Nations, General Assembly, Annual Report of the Secretary-General on the Work of the Organization, 1 July 1951-30 June 1952 (A/2141). New York, 1952.

e. Judicial cases.

Great Britain, Court of Quarter Sessions of the Peace (Lincolnshire), Records of Some Sessions of the Peace in Lincolnshire, 1360-1375, ed. Rosamond Sillem . . . , Vol. XXX of the Lincoln Record Society, Publications. Hereford: Hereford Times, Ltd., 1936. xcii, 325 pp.

Herold, David E., Defendant, The Assassination of President Lincoln and the Trial of the Conspirators David E. Herold, Mary E. Surratt, Lewis Payne, George A. Atzerodt, Edward Spangler, Samuel A Mudd, Samuel Arnold, Michael O'Laughlin . . . , comp. and arr. by Benn Pitman, recorder to the Commission. Cincinnati & New York: Moore, Wilstach & Baldwin, 1865. xvi, 17-421 pp. Illus., maps.

See also 5-D-11, below.

3. Articles and essays.

Knight, John, "Matchless Magellan: The Story of a Voyage," The Middle States Historical Journal, XXXII (Apr. 1927), 508-27.

Or if no month is given — XXXII, No. 3 (1927); or if published more frequently — XXXII (15 Apr. 1927), 508-27.

Knight, John, "Magellan's Character," The Journal of the Central Historical Association, XI (May 1962), 127-39 — or alternatively, and more logically, only for a periodical with a title specifically stipulating the sponsoring organization — The Central Historical Association, Journal, XI (May 1962) 127-39. But in this case be consistent.

Knight, John, "Ferdinand Magellan," pp. 347-79 in The Great Explorers, ed. James Charles Squire. New York: Brown Co., 1927.

Knight, John, "Ferdinand Magellan," pp. 347-79 in The Spanish Adventurers, ed. James Charles Squire, Vol. IV of The Saga of Mankind, ed. George D. Page. New York: Brown Co., 1927.

Knight, John, "Columbus, Christopher," Special Encyclopedia, II, 200-205, ed. James Charles Squire. Prairie City, Mo.: Pink & White, Inc., 1923.

Knight, John, "Vasco da Gama," General Encyclopaedia, 12th ed.; XXXI, 311-15. No other publication data are needed for a well known encyclopedia.

4. Book reviews.

Page, George D., Review of The History of Exploration in America, by John Knight, The Middle States Historical Journal, XXXIII (Apr. 1928), 400-402.

5. Unpublished studies.

Page, George Dogberry, Jr., "London Sailors under Henry VIII: A Study of Their Origins." Unpublished Ph.D. dissertation [or MS M. A. thesis], Central University of America, 1955. ix, 139 pp.

6. Newspapers.

The Prairie City (Missouri) Cyclone.

Expresses the views of the editor and publisher, John Ritter, an uncompromising Greenbacker who opposed even a silver supported currency. Declining advertisements by merchants suggest economic pressure against him.

The (London) Times, 1 June 1892-30 Nov. 1893.

The New York Times, 1 June-30 Nov. 1892.

Older, Jonathan, "Silver Thorns," in The Prairie City (Missouri) Cyclone, 24 July 1896. By-line article.

Younger, Jack, "Silver Thorns," letter, Confederate Cross Roads, Missouri, 27 July 1896, to the editor, in The [Prairie City, Missouri] Farmer's Friend, 1 Aug. 1896.

If the place of publication is not indicated in the title but is given elsewhere in the newspaper, enclose it in parentheses; if it has to be determined by additional research, place it in brackets. If your investigation covers many newspapers, it may be convenient for you to group them by areas in your bibliography. In this case you may not need to insert the place of publication in the title.

7. Manuscript collections.

Knight, John, MSS. Library of Congress. 27 boxes, approximately 12,000 letters, 1871-1905, 2 letter press books, 1884-87, and diary, 1901-1902.

Important for picture of student and professorial life of period. Unfortunately the correspondence relating to Professor Knight's quarrel with President George Knabe of Midwest College appears to have been removed, and probably destroyed, before the collection was deposited in the Library of Congress.

Squire, James Charles, MSS Diary, 19 Mar. 1905-17 Feb. 1943. Central University of America Library. 38 vols. Used by permission of Mrs. James Charles Squire.

Census, Bureau of the, Population Schedules, 7th Census, 1850, Illinois. National Archives. In 24 bound vols., arranged alphabetically by counties.

State, Department of, Consular Dispatches, Manila. National Archives. 13 vols., 1817-99.

State, Department of, Decimal File 862.00, 1910-29. National Archives.

Navy Department, Area 9 File, Record Group 45. National Archives.

Germany, Foreign Ministry Archives, Der Weltkrieg Nr. 15 Geheim: Material zu den Friedensverhandlungen, Vols. 2-4, 1 Aug. 1916-31 Dec. 1917. Bonn. Also microfilm in U. S. National Archives.

Consult the repository in which the collection is located concerning the type of identification that will enable anyone to go immediately to it. (See 5-D-7, final paragraph, below.)

8. Personal correspondence.

Knight, John, 6 letters, Feb.-Apr. 1956, to the author.

9. Oral interviews.

Knight, John, personal interview, New York, 19 Mar. 1956, with the author.

James C. Squire Manufacturing Co., Prairie City, Missouri. Personal interview with James Charles Squire, Jr., President, at Widget Manufacturers of America National Convention, Chicago, 3 Oct. 1956.

D. FOOTNOTES

Footnotes are of three types, although they appear together without distinction. They are: (1) Explanatory notes, consisting of comments or the discussion of somewhat digressive matters which you feel it necessary to deal with without unnecessarily impeding the flow of your main treatment. These should be used sparingly. In general, if a subject cannot be fitted smoothly into your narrative, it is better to omit it altogether. There are few things more annoying than attempting to follow the course of a thin stream of narrative through a morass of explanatory footnotes. In the hands of a skilled writer footnote comments can sometimes be used to spice the narrative. A prime example is Robert L. Duffus, *The Innocents at Cedro,* in which humorous asides add measurably to the book's nostalgic charm. (2) Cross references to other parts of your narrative or to other footnotes are useful devices wherever it is necessary to treat different aspects of the same topic at two or more points in the development of your subject. (But try not to put your reader in the position where he is incessantly having to turn back and forth.) You can often fit such notes into your text, itself, enclosed in parentheses. (3) Every direct quotation, **each** statement of fact that is not generally known or self-evident, and any interpretation borrowed from another source *must* be indicated in some fashion. This is by far the most necessary function of footnotes, enabling the reader to check the accuracy and justification of anything whatsoever that you include in your treatise. A footnote number should appear in your text immediately following the statement that you must vouch for, even if in the midst of a sentence, and should be raised one-half space. If all the matter in a paragraph or longer section is derived from the same source or sources, one footnote will often suffice for the whole. Footnotes should be numbered consecutively for each chapter, or for the entire paper if it is a short one, rather than starting afresh with each page. Even in the case of reference citations it is often possible to indicate your source in the body of the text, even strengthening the latter thereby, setting off the specific page or pages referred to by the use of commas or parentheses.

Footnotes are normally grouped at the bottom of the page preceded by the appropriate number (often raised one-half space), and separated from the text by a solid line of type from margin to margin. For a textbook they might be cited at the end of a chapter, and for a book intended for the general public at the back of the book — especially if they are very extensive. (See par. 5-E-15, below.) They should be single spaced, in contrast to your text which would be double spaced; but with double spacing between the footnote paragraphs. If the numbered references are brief, two or more may be put on the same line. When the material in your text is derived from several sources that cannot readily be separated from each other in proper sequence, you may group them all in one footnote, separated by semicolons. A long footnote may, if necessary, be completed at the bottom of the next page before the next footnote, if there is one there.

In all but your final draft, however, it is advisable to place the footnote on the next line immediately following the portion of the text to which it refers, drawing lines from margin to margin both before and after the footnote to separate it from the text. In this case it is best to type it double spaced to facilitate corrections. A blank space should be left for the appropriate number in both the text and note so that you can conveniently insert the numbers in your final draft. (See 5-A-4, second paragraph, above.)

In form, footnote references differ in four respects from bibliographical references: (1) you give the author's name in its regular order, since it will not be filed or listed alphabetically; (2) you place the publishing data in parentheses in order to avoid any confusion with the citation of page numbers; (3) you cite the specific page, or pages, from which the note is taken; and (4) you omit all of the supplemental information indicated after the date of publication in the bibliographical reference. In citing the derivation of your information for the first time in each chapter (as well as in the headings for your content notes) follow the models set forth below.

1. Books.

John Knight, The <u>History</u> <u>of</u> <u>Exploration</u> <u>in</u> <u>America</u> (New York: Brown Co., 1927), p. 7. — or pp. 1, 7, 70-77, 71-72, 703-707, 708-15, 722-27, 738-39, 797-811; or i-iii; or I, 7; or Ch. V.

Johann Ritter, The History of Exploration in America, trans.
James Charles Squire (3d ed.; New York: Brown Co., 1927), II, 7,
23-25.

The presence of a volume number may be considered as making the inclusion
of the abbreviation for page unnecessary.

John Knight, The History of Exploration in America: An Adventure
during Four Centuries, Vol. IV of The Saga of Mankind, ed. James
Charles Squire (New York: Brown Co., 1927), pp. 52-57.

Johannes Knyghte, Historie of New Worlde Exploration (London, 1621),
p. 37, in [or — quoted in] James Charles Squire, The Age of Discovery (New
York: Brown Co., 1928), p. 101. When the original is not available to you.

If the author and title, or any other parts of the necessary information, are
given in the text they need not be repeated in the footnote. Thus

(New York: Brown Co., 1927), p. 7.

2. Public documents.

U. S., Congress, Senate, Committee on Education and Labor, Vio-
lations of Free Speech and Rights of Labor: Industrial Munitions.
(76th Cong., 1st sess., Senate Report 6, part 3, March 20 [legis-
lative day March 16], 1939, pursuant to Senate Resolution 266, 74th
Cong.) (Washington: Government Printing Office, 1939), pp. 107-15.
(Hereinafter referred to as Sen. Rept. 6.)

U. S., War Department, The War of the Rebellion: A Compilation of
the Official Records of the Union and Confederate Armies (hereinafter referred to as O. R.), Ser. I. Vol. XLI, pt. 2 (Washington:
Government Printing Office, 1892), p. 455, Maj. Gen. William Starke
Rosecrans, Commanding, Department of Missouri, St. Louis, 29 July
1864, to Governor Richard Yates, Springfield, Illinois.

3. Articles and essays.

John Knight, "Matchless Magellan: The Story of a Voyage," The
Middle States Historical Journal, XXXII (Apr. 1927), 510.

John Knight, "Ferdinand Magellan," in The Great Explorers, ed.
James Charles Squire (New York: Brown Co., 1927), p. 362.

4. Book reviews.

George D. Page, Review of The History of Exploration in America,
by John Knight, The Middle States Historical Journal, XXXIII (Apr.
1928), 401.

5. Unpublished studies.

George Dogberry Page, Jr., "London Sailors under Henry VIII: A
Study of Their Origins" (unpublished [or MS] Ph.D. dissertation,
Central University of America, 1955), p. 92.

6. Newspapers.

The New York Times, 19 Mar. 1956, pp. 1, 4. [Or C-14, or VI-7.]

The Prairie City (Missouri) Cyclone, 28 Feb. 1958, p. 3. It is general practice not to give page references for small newspapers, but it is a timesaving convenience to the reader that requires little extra effort by the author.

7. Manuscript collections.

Because the reader's interest will be concentrated upon a particular item instead of a collection as a whole, the footnote citation for a manuscript is given in substantially reverse order of the form employed in listing a manuscript collection in your bibliography. Check from internal evidence to determine if letters of January and early February have been absent-mindedly dated as of the preceding year.

James Charles Squire, New York, 19 Mar. 1897, letter to John Knight, Prairie City, Missouri, File Box 17, John Knight MSS, Library of Congress.

Entry of 13 Aug. 1927, James Charles Squire MS Diary, Vol. 22, Central University of America Library.

Consul Alexander R. Webb, 26 July 1891, to Assistant Secretary Wharton, Consular Dispatches, Manila, Vol. 12, Department of State, National Archives. Titles, place, and date may be omitted if made clear by the text. Since the number of boxes or volumes of collections in public repositories often runs to over one hundred, it is, for consistency, generally advisable to employ Arabic numerals throughout.

Ambassador William E. Dodd, Berlin, 4 Nov. 1933, to Secretary Hull, 862.00/3131, Department of State, National Archives.

Secretary Welles, Washington, 3 Aug. 1865, telegram to Rear Admiral Pearson, Area 9 File, Record Group 45, Navy Department, National Archives.

Minister Henry Lane Wilson, 9 July 1898, to Secretary Day (received 12 Aug.), Dispatches, Chile, Vol. 46, Department of State, National Archives.

Hindenburg, 5 Apr. 1917, letter to Bethmann-Hollweg, Weltkrieg 15 Geheim (hereinafter referred to as WK 15 Geh.), Vol. 2, German Foreign Ministry, Bonn (hereinafter referred to as GFM); microfilm 1498/3107H/ D627623 of U. S. National Archives. (The last three sets of numbers refer to microfilm reel, serial, and frame.)

Transcribed long-distance telephone conversation between Commander Clover and Charles R. Flint, 3 p.m., Wed., 30 Mar. 1898, envelope "AY -- Purchase of Vessels for the Use of the U. S. Navy, 1898," Record Group 45, Navy Department, National Archives.

Consult the repository for the matter to be included in your reference which will enable your reader to go with the greatest possible convenience to the precise letter or document you cite. See, for example, *Information for*

Searchers Citing Records in the National Archives (Washington: National Archives, 1957), 4 pp.

8. Personal correspondence.

John Knight, New York, letter, 19 Mar. 1956, to the author.

9. Oral interviews.

James Charles Squire, Jr., President, James C. Squire Manufacturing Co., Prairie City, Missouri, personal interview with the author at Widget Manufacturers of America National Convention, Chicago, 3 Oct. 1956.

10. Classical references.

As a general rule you will cite materials in this field in the forms previously suggested; but since most surviving Classical and Medieval sources are well known to specialists in those fields, it is common practice to refer to them by conventionalized contractions. (See *American Journal of Archaeology*, LIV [July 1950], 268–72; LVI [Jan. 1952], 1–7.) The numerals in the examples below indicate divisions and subdivisions of the work cited in descending order in accordance with its particular arrangement: book, chapter, section, paragraph, verse, sentence, or line. Brackets are used here to indicate a parenthesis within a parenthesis.

Pliny Nat. hist. 5.1.12.

Galen De anat. adminst. (Kuhn) 2.217, 224-25.   Indicates edition.

Lactanius Divin. instit. 5.2-3.

Appian Mith. 8.

Isaiah 29.21.   Where only a single work by an author survives, it is not necessary to give the title. Theological writers commonly use colons between the numbers.

Herod. 2.102.   Even the names of particularly familiar authors may be abbreviated.

11. Legal citations.

For the complexities in this field it is advisable to consult *A Uniform System of Citation: Form of Citation and Abbreviations.* 10th ed.; Cambridge, Mass.: Harvard Law Review Assoc., c. 1958. iv, 124 pp. Index.

Most commonly cited in this special manner by the general historian would be court decisions, as

Dartmouth College v. Woodward, 17 U. S. (4 Wheat.) 518 (1819).
which identifies a decision of the Supreme Court of the United States by reference to the plaintiff and defendant, the volume, the report editor (a practice abandoned in 1875), page, and date. The name of the reporter (Wheaton) in this case is customarily abbreviated.

Hemphill v. Wabash R. R. Co., 209 F.2d 768 (7th Cir. 1954), cert denied, 374 U. S. 954 (1954). Refers to the volume in the *Federal Reporter*, 2d series, and page number, in which a decision of the 7th Circuit Court of Appeals is given, a decision which the Supreme Court refused to review, as requested under a writ of certiorari, as recorded by reference to the appropriate indicated volume and page of the *Supreme Court Reporter*. The citation indicated that both actions took place in 1954. Since 1932 U. S. district court decisions have been separately reported in the *Federal Supplement* — abbreviation F. Supp. If a case is referred to in the body of your text it would be underscored (italicized in print) — Hemphill v. Wabash R. R. Co.

Malanchuk v. St. Mary's Greek Catholic Church, 336 Pa. 385, 399, 9 A.2d 350, 356 (1939). This citation gives the volume number, together with the beginning page of the case and the specific page thereof to which reference is made, and the year in both the official state report and in the unofficial but more widely distributed *Atlantic Reporter*, 2d series. (The standard abbreviation for the first series is Atl.)

Savant v. Superior Coal Co., 5 Ill. App. 2d 109, 125 N.E.2d 148 (1955). Refers to volume of state court reports, 2d series, the page number, and the additional reference to the unofficial *North Eastern Reporter*.

Dochkus v. Lithuanian Benefit Soc'y, 206 Pa. 25, 55 Atl. 779 (1903). Note use of abbreviation.

Case of S. S. "Wimbledon," Permanent Court of International Justice (commonly and hereinafter as P. C. I. J.), Ser. A., No. 1 (1923), pp. 23-28.

New York Laws 1875, c. 74 § 4. In indicating chapter and section the conventional symbol for the latter may be made on a typewriter not specially equipped with it by superimposing one letter *s*, half raised, upon another; or one may simply use a standard abbreviation — sect. — see next item.

Transportation Act of 1920, 41 Stat. 477 (1920), as amended 49 U.S.C., sect. 1 (18) (1958). Refers to volume and page number in the federal *Statutes at Large* and in the *United States Code,* respectively.

12. Additional citations in a chapter.

After you have cited a book or other reference by its full title and publishing information in accordance with the appropriate form shown above, you will thereafter refer to it throughout a chapter or short paper in a briefer form. Recent practice is increasingly toward using a "short form," thus:

Knight, History of Exploration, p. 7.

Knight, "Matchless Magellan," pp. 511-12.

Grant, City Point, 13 Sept. 1864, to Stanton, O. R., Ser. III, Vol. IV, 712-13.

Squire, London, 3 Oct. 1897, to Knight, Prairie City, Knight MSS.

The short form (which must be used anyway in those instances where one has included two or more works by the same author) has the additional advantage of making it easier for the reader to recall the work as previously cited. Where there are two or more authors with the same surname, they will be additionally identified by their first names or initials. Titles that are awkward to abbreviate may be given some rather arbitrary designation, with a note appended to the first citation, such as — (hereinafter referred to as Sen. Rept. 6) — for the first citation contained in 5-D-2, above. In a long article, without a bibliography, it may be helpful to give a cross reference to the first, complete citation.

The Latin form, using abbreviations, is, however, still widely used. Its advantage is its brevity. It would be as follows:

Knight, op. cit., p. 7.

Or, if one is referring to precisely the same pages as before, including an entire article or essay, he might use the form

Knight, loc. cit.

These are abbreviations, respectively, of *opere citato* (in the work cited) and *loco citato* (in the place cited).

There is one Latin form, from *ibidem, meaning* "in the same place," that will probably continue to be used for its convenience when citing a work again *immediately* after it has been referred to in the previous footnote:

Ibid.   Means not only the same title but same pages.

Ibid., pp. 101-107.   Means same title but different pages.

Other frequently encountered abbreviations and Latin words, of which most of those in Latin are now often used in the form of their English equivalents, are:

c.	(copyright)
ca.	(*circa* — at or near a given date)
cf.	(*confer* — compare with or consult)
e. g.	(*exempli gratia* — for example)
et al.	(*et alii* — and others)
et seq.	(*et sequens* — and following)
ff.	(pages following)
id.	(*idem* — the same)
i. e.	(*id est* — that is)
infra	(below, later on in the text)
MS	(one manuscript, or used as adjective)
MSS	(more than one manuscript, usually a collection, as — John Knight MSS, Library of Congress)
n.	(note)
passim	(here and there)
q. v.	(*quod vide* — which see)
sic	(thus — to show that a statement is correctly quoted, although original is erroneous)
supra	(above — earlier in the text)
vide	(see)

E. FINAL ARRANGEMENT

A published book might conceivably include all of the following, and perhaps still other parts; but your own work, if it is a term paper or thesis, will probably contain only those items preceded by asterisks. Those preceded by two asterisks are essential. Articles in periodicals may in some degree informally reflect much the same general order.

★1. Blank page.

2. Half title.

3. Series title.

★★4. Title page. Each line on this page should be equally balanced on each side of an imaginary perpendicular line down the middle of the page. First comes your title and your subtitle, if any, without a period at the end. If the subtitle is placed on a second line, there is no punctuation after the title. Halfway down the page comes your full name, preceded by "by" and followed, if a thesis or dissertation, by your previous degree(s), together with granting institution and year of award. You will indicate at the bottom of the page the course for which it is a term paper, or if a thesis the institution, degree, and date thereof as stipulated by the practices of the college in which you are enrolled. For example,

LONDON SAILORS UNDER HENRY VIII
A STUDY OF THEIR ORIGINS

by

George Dogberry Page, Jr.
A. B., 1954, Midwest College

A thesis submitted to the Graduate Faculty of Arts and Letters of the Central University of America in partial satisfaction of the requirements for the degree of Master of Arts in History.

June 1955

Thesis directed by John Knight, Ph. D.

or whatever other form may be required by your institution.

If it were a published book, the material following the name of the author might be simply

New York
Brown Co., Inc.
1927

5. Copyright information.

6. Dedication. To be brief and dignified, without either cloying sentimentality or ingratiating flattery, if used at all.

7. Preface. A vestige of the old "apology" by the author, it can be used briefly either by the author, the editor of the series if the work is a volume in such a series, or some other person to state the circumstances that led to the undertaking and the limitations that have necessarily been placed upon its scope. Its import may very well be carried over to the Introduction (5-E-13, below.)

8. Acknowledgments. These should include only those persons and institutions who have given you substantial assistance, and generally in order of the value of their aid, not of their standing in the profession. Never use them to imply that your work enjoys impressive sponsorship. They may be included in the Preface (5-E-7, above) or as an appendix (5-E-16, below). Don't forget the librarian or archivist who has helped you locate material.

★★9. Table of contents. May be either of two types:
    a. Chapter titles, perhaps in shortened form.
    b. Chapter titles, plus list of topics covered in each. Usually found in textbooks. That used in this booklet is, because of its intended use, a particularly elaborate form which also serves in lieu of an index.

★10. List of maps.

★11. List of illustrations.

★12. List of charts and tables.

★13. Introduction. In it you indicate the setting of your study, your objectives, and the materials and techniques you have employed. It may constitute the opening section of your first chapter instead of being set apart.

★★14. The text, by chapters. With footnotes at bottom of appropriate pages.

15. Reference notes. Employed where the exigencies of publication, usually for a more general audience, require segregation at the end of the volume of the citations that would otherwise be given in footnotes. In this case be sure to give both the chapter number and title at the beginning of each section. It is a further convenience to your reader if you place the page numbers in the text to which the notes refer at the top of each page of reference notes.

★16. Appendix or appendices, if any. Here you may reproduce some vital source material to which the reader would not otherwise have access. You may also include what are, in effect, short subordinate essays on related matters that are too specialized for adequate treatment in the body of the text and too lengthy for convenient inclusion in a footnote.

★★17. Annotated bibliography. The appropriate forms, including a suggestion for the type of annotative comments you should include, are given in 5-C, above. Works of lesser importance to your study may be described in a word or brief phrase. All items should be listed alphabetically, according to the author's last name, or, if there is no author or editor, by the first word of the title (except *a, an,* or *the,* or the equivalent in a foreign language), arranged under something like the following headings. If there are few items in any section, it may be consolidated with some other appropriate section; but sources and secondary works should generally be separated.

a. Sources.

(1) *Manuscripts,* personal correspondence, and oral interviews.

(2) Published *public documents.*

(3) *Newspapers.* If very numerous may be subdivided by nations, states, cities, or political affiliations. Frequently it may be desirable to indicate the period or issues consulted.

(4) *Books, articles,* book reviews, and unpublished studies that are classifiable as sources. Sources, or primary materials, are those that for the particular study in which you are engaged provide ear- and eyewitness accounts or the nearest approximation thereto that you can obtain. The line between sources and secondary works must be drawn functionally for each investigation. For example, William E. Dodd's biography, *Woodrow Wilson and His Work,* would be a primary source for a study of Professor Dodd as an historian, but a secondary work for a study of President Wilson. A primary source (which may simply be called a source) does *not* receive its classification from the fact that it was of primary importance or helpfulness in your study, nor is a secondary work necessarily one that was peripheral to your undertaking. This is emphasized as a common misunderstanding among beginners.

b. Secondary works. These will in most cases also consist of books, articles, book reviews, unpublished dissertations, etc. They will generally be listed together, whether published or unpublished, in alphabetical order without subdivision.

18. Index. This can be prepared quite easily by using the page proof of a book, starting with the first page and making out a 3×5, 4×6, or 5×8 inch card for each person, event, or topic of importance that you have touched upon. Keep in alphabetical order in a file box, and record the page number each time the name or topic appears. Larger items may be broken into subheadings.

6 COMMUNICATION

It takes two to speak the truth —
one to speak, and another to hear.
Thoreau, *A Week on the Concord and*
Merrimac Rivers, "Wednesday."

You have undoubtedly experienced both difficulty and compensating satisfaction as you have searched out and digested the material of your investigation. Now, as you set about communicating the significance of your discoveries to someone else, these feelings will reach their climax. Your research that began with a methodology that was essentially scientific will now rise to the level of an art.

1. Elements of style.

a. Words. A good dictionary or thesaurus will aid you in phrasing the exact meaning you wish to convey and in finding synonyms for overworked expressions. A fresh direction of approach to your line of thought may help you to eliminate clichés; and a walk about the room or a stroll around the block is sometimes the best way of finding the precise expression that fits your thought. If you must break a word at the end of a line, follow proper syllabification — taking particular care in the case of proper names. Never leave a single letter from a word standing alone.

b. Sentences. Short, simple, declarative sentences that are predominantly in the active voice — but sufficiently varied to avoid monotony — should be the workhorses of your narration. Use adjectives sparingly, adverbs scarcely less so, and only when you are confident that they will stimulate rather than becloud the reader's imagination. Narration takes precedence over description, and both over prolonged commentary. You can normally gain in clarity by bringing as closely together as possible adjectives and the nouns which they describe, adverbs and the verbs they modify, and qualifying phrases or clauses and the things to which they relate. An occasional balanced sentence can, where appropriate, provide a touch of classical dignity, or an inverted one lead the way to a climax. Standard rules of punctuation serve, through habituated usage, as directional signs that help the reader to follow the nuances of your meaning. Often, however, you must exercise a choice as to whether a comma, dash, semicolon, or a period — each of them able to check the eye of the reader as an inflection of the voice or a pause does for the ear — best serves your purpose at any given point.[12] The skilled and experienced writer can make his

---

12 Useful references concerning matters of grammatical construction include Turabain, *Manual* (see footnote 11, above) and Edwin Campbell Woolley, Franklin W. Scott, and Frederick Bracher, *College Handbook of Composition* (6th ed., rev.; Boston, etc.: D. C. Heath & Co. c. 1958), 474 pp.; William Strunk, Jr. and Elwyn Brooks White, *The Elements of Style*

own exceptions to the rules. There is a military adage that "a good general does not place his army with its back to a river, unless he is of a mind to do so." The significant word here is "mind," indicating that there should be a good reason for an action contrary to accepted practice. But the beginner should be wary of incautious experimentation.

c. **Paragraphs.** In opening a paragraph, a topic sentence should serve as a bridge from the preceding paragraph — sometimes by echoing a key word or concept — and should announce the essence of what is to follow. The rest of the paragraph should then prove the thesis of the opening statement. The concluding sentence should be a summary or comment that serves as an approach to the next bridge. Occasionally it may offer a flourish or peroration on a rising note to drive home an idea. The opening and closing chapters of a book, together with the first and last paragraphs of each of the other chapters and the topic and concluding sentences of each of the other paragraphs — all in their proper sequence — should, ideally, state the essence of the book in intelligible form. Use properly documented quotations where they will be most apt. Exercise the strictest economy of expression that will suffice to convey your full meaning. It is axiomatic that the more thoroughly you have mastered your subject, the more succinctly you can express it. Figures of speech and flecks of color can tone up a narrative; but immoderate indulgence arouses a distaste comparable to that of a banquet consisting entirely of pastries. Revision and rewriting consist largely of excision and condensation while, at the same time, bringing out the deeper meanings and larger implications of your subject. When you doubt the need for any word, phrase, or paragraph, eliminate it.

d. **Chapters.** Each chapter, like an article in a periodical, is a miniature book. At the same time it must advance the message of the book as a whole.

e. **Special nomenclature.** Be sure to follow accepted forms for such titles as "Reverend" and "Honorable" (or their abbreviations "Rev." and "Hon.") which are always preceded by the word "the," followed by a secondary title thus — the Rev. Mr. (or Dr., or John) Knight. Ascertain the correct form of address for the higher clergy of any church. Present-day naval practice is invariably to *omit* the word "the" before ships' names. There is a standard form of reference, often abbreviated, for military units — Co. A, 2d Bn., 136th Arty.

(rev. ed.; New York: Macmillan Co., c. 1959), xiv, 71 pp.; Henry Watson Fowler, *A Dictionary of Modern English Usage* (Oxford: Clarendon Press, 1926); Margaret Nicholson, *A Dictionary of American-English Usage Based on Fowler's Modern English Usage* (New York: Oxford University Press, 1957); and Herbert William Horwill, *A Dictionary of Modern American Usage* (ibid., 1935) are all helpful in the development of exactitude in language. Albert H. Marckwardt, *American English* (ibid., 1958) is a useful introduction. Bergen Evans and Cornelia Evans, *A Dictionary of Contemporary American Usage* (New York: Random House, c. 1957) offers a somewhat more flexible approach than do works that follow the lead of Fowler. Henry M. Silver, "Putting It on Paper," *PMLA*, LXV (Apr. 1950), 9–20, and *The New York Times Style Book*, ed. Lewis Jordan (New York: McGraw-Hill, 1962), 124 pp., are excellent on the preparation of manuscript for publication. For the way in which one especially felicitous writer developed his style see Charlotte Watkins Smith, "Carl Becker: The Historian as a Literary Craftsman," *William and Mary Quarterly*, Ser. III, Vol. IX (July 1952), 291–316, and her *Carl Becker: On History and the Climate of Opinion* (Ithaca: Cornell University Press, 1956, xi, 225 pp.)

Regt., 29th Inf. Div., V Corps, First Army, or First U. S. Army. (See U. S., Department of the Army, Office of Military History, *Style Manual for Military History*. Washington, 1959. ii, 51 pp. Mimeographed.) Underscore (in print italicized) names of plays and set the names of characters therein in quotation marks. Do not confuse the old symbol (known as a "thorn") for "th" with the letter "y." The old English "ye" is the modern "you"; but the practice of early printers of using the letter "y" as a substitute for the thorn has led to confusion. Distinguish between a title of nobility — John, Lord Knightsbridge, for the baron or earl of Knightsbridge, with a "courtesy title" — Lord John Knight, borne by a younger son. (See Valentine Heywood, *British Titles* . . . . London: A. C. Black, c. 1953.)

f. Numerals. In your text you should, as a rule, spell out numbers of one or two digits, but use numerals for those running to three or more. Also spell out a number at the beginning of a sentence and, in this case, all subsequent numbers in the sentence or following closely thereafter; or, preferably, contrive to begin the sentence with another word. In any form of tabulation or in groups containing numbers both over and under three digits, use Arabic numerals throughout. Centuries may be referred to either by numeral or in written form — 14th century or fourteenth century (sometimes capitalized, if one chooses, as 14th Century or Fourteenth Century) — so long as you are consistent.

2. Learning by example. All thinking creatures learn by observation, imitation, experimentation, and constant practice. Cultivate a discriminating selectivity. Strive to improve your taste to the point where it automatically rejects the meretricious and banal. Turn to the vast treasure house of all past world literature for models to be found in both historical and imaginative writing. Remember the example of young Benjamin Franklin, forced to abandon the hope of grammar school and college, who found in the *Spectator* papers an example of urbane incisiveness (not unlike the style that characterizes today's *The New Yorker*) that helped him to develop one of the most effective writing styles in an age of literary elegance. Concentrate upon the writers who are best suited to point the way to your own fullest potentialities.

3. Practice makes — . There is no substitute for writing and rewriting, for continually rising to the challenge of new undertakings. Get into the habit of writing and publishing before the habit of not writing becomes fixed.

Strive for constant improvement. It often helps to come back, after an interval of time, to that which you have previously written so that you may read it with something of the critical eye of a stranger and thus more readily detect any weakness of thought or awkwardness of expression. You will gradually develop a trained eye and "inner ear" that will enable you to recognize, in rereading your successive drafts, "the one best way" to evolve and express your thought. There is drudgery in research and writing, as in any undertaking. But it is more than compensated for by those exhilarating periods, which will increase as you acquire a mastery of your field and a facility of expression, when the ideas and phrases flow easily from your mind and pen. Whatever the material compensation, the psychic rewards are beyond price. There is, above all, the satisfaction of coming to a better understanding of the world about you — and hence of yourself. Thus can you hope, both through the discovery of things previously unknown and in the manner in which you live, to make a contribution, however modest, to the truth that is history.

Courtesy of *The Washington Post and Times-Herald* and permission of United Features Syndicate.